Supplement

ZEITSCHRIFT FÜR PSYCHOLOGIE

mit Zeitschrift für angewandte Psychologie

MACINTER

Selected papers from workshops organized by the Network on Man-Computer Interaction Research (MACINTER) of the International Union of Psychological Science (IUPsyS)

Herausgegeben von Friedhart Klix und Hartmut Wandke

JOHANN AMBROSIUS BARTH LEIPZIG

ZEITSCHRIFT FÜR PSYCHOLOGIE
mit Zeitschrift für angewandte Psychologie

Schriftleitung: Friedhart Klix, Berlin

Redaktion: Jürgen Mehl, Berlin

Supplement 9 (1987)

MACINTER

Selected papers from workshops organized by the Network of Man-Computer Interaction Research (MACINTER) of the International Union of Psychological Science (IUPsyS)

Herausgegeben von
Friedhart Klix und Hartmut Wandke

Mit 42 Abbildungen

JOHANN AMBROSIUS BARTH 1987

Verlag: Johann Ambrosius Barth, Salomonstr. 18 b, Leipzig, DDR – 7010, Ruf 70 131
Schriftleitung: Prof. Dr. F. Klix, Sektion Psychologie der Humboldt-Universität, Oranienburger Str. 18, Berlin, DDR – 1020
Veröffentlicht unter der Lizenznummer 1394 des Presseamtes beim Vorsitzenden des Ministerrates der DDR
Satz und Druck: Druckhaus Karl-Marx-Stadt, Betrieb Druckerei Annaberg-Buchholz, Markt 8, Annaberg-Buchholz, DDR – 9300
AN (EDV) 87518
DDR 01200, Ausland 24,– DM

Content

Preface 5

Wandke, H.; Wetzenstein-Ollenschläger, E. (Berlin/GDR). Human-computer interface design considering semantic aspects. With 12 fig. 7

Muthig, K. P.; Reinhardt, G. (Heidelberg/FDR). Comparison of iconic and verbal editor commands: some results from scanning studies. With 3 fig. 21

Wandmacher, J.; Müller, U. (Darmstadt/FDR). On the usability of verbal and iconic command representations. With 4 fig. 35

van der Veern, G. E.; Felt, M. A. M.; von Muylwijk, B.; van Biene, R. J. (Amsterdam/The Netherlands). Learning an office system – a field study on the development of mental models. With 11 fig. 46

Waern, Y.;, Rabenius, L. (Stockholm/Sweden). On the role of models in the instruction of novice users of a word processing system. 59

Schindler, R. (Berlin/GDR). Psychological aspects of training of users in interactive computer systems. With 5 fig. 74

Wetzenstein-Ollenschläger, Elke; Krause, B.; Hagendorf, H. (Berlin/GDR). Approaches for analysing and designing computer aided problem solving processes. With 6 fig. 82

Preface

Man-computer interaction research is an area of psychological investigation that has received more and more attention over the last seven or eight years, in terms of publications, conferences, journals, newsletters, organizations, etc.

Man-Computer Interaction Research (MACINTER) is also the name of a network of the International Union of Psychological Science (IUPsyS). The network started to work in 1984 with a first meeting of interested psychologists in Berlin, German Democratic Republic. The proceedings of that First Network Seminar were published under the title of MACINTER I by North-Holland in 1986.

During the meeting, the participants decided to organize smaller workshops with more specific subjects of human-computer interaction, in the next two or three years.

Two MACINTER workshops were held in 1985.

The first was held on the occasion of the VIIth Meeting of Psychologists from the Danubian Countries in Varna (Bulgaria), September 28, 1985. (In spite of the name of the conference, participation was not restricted to Danubian countries.) The subject of the workshop was Knowledge Acquisition and Measurement of Mental Load in Man-Computer Interaction. The programme was drawn up by the MACINTER office in close cooperation with the local organizer, Ph. Genov (Sofia). Chairman of the meeting was F. Klix (Berlin, GDR).

The second workshop was held one day before the conference on Software Ergonomics '85 was opened, on September 23, 1985. The conference was organized by the German Chapter of the Association for Computing Machinery (ACM). It took place in Stuttgart (Federal Republic of Germany).

The MACINTER workshop was devoted to the subject of Knowledge and Visual Information Representation in Man-Computer Interaction. It was organized and chaired by M. Tauber and G. Rohr (both Heidelberg, FRG).

The contributions to this supplement volume are revised versions of papers read at both MACINTER workshops.

What is the specific approach of MACINTER as compared with other international organizations dealing with issues of human-computer interaction? We believe that the main task of MACINTER is to be a medium of information exchange on, and (as far as possible) for, the stimulation of psychological research as a basis for the solution of design problems.

The usual starting point of many investigations concerning human-computer interaction issues is system design, from which one goes backwards to look for principles of software ergonomics (standards, guidelines etc.) or results of applied psychology (s. fig. 1).

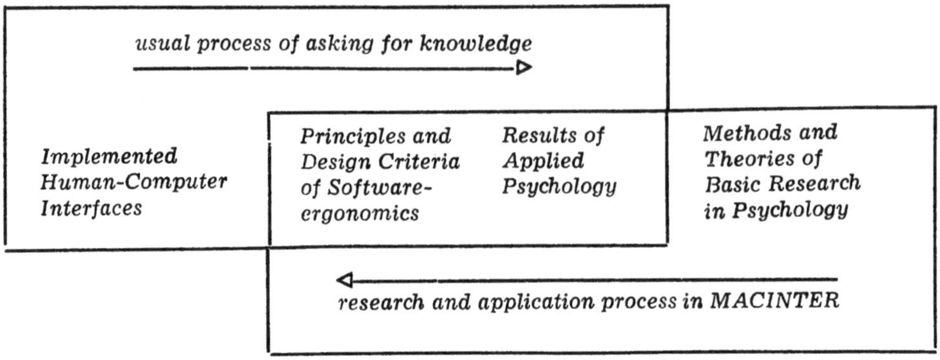

Fig. 1. Steps of psychological research in Human-Computer Interaction

In contrast, we psychologists should start from basic psychology (especially from cognitive psychology); and our task is to provide the software engineers with psychological theories, models and data applicable in system design. This is a forward strategy: looking for system design aspects in which psychological knowledge is needed.

Psychological research cannot, of course, be carried out without any (real or mock-up) systems being used. But they serve as means or instruments for experiments, rather than subjects of research.

So, the articles of this volume should be seen as contributions to our understanding of how people process information when interacting with a computer, not as direct answers to the question of how to build up user interfaces.

We gratefully acknowledge the efforts of the workshop organizers and we wish to thank especially the participants of the workshop who were kind enough to "brush up" their papers for publication in the special MACINTER issue of the supplement series of Zeitschrift für Psychologie.

F. Klix and H. Wandke

From the Department of Psychology, Humboldt University Berlin, GDR

Human-computer interface design considering semantic aspects

By H. Wandke and Elke Wetzenstein-Ollenschläger

With 12 figures

Introduction

Designing the interface of a human-computer system is a challenge for psychology and a touchstone of its ability to apply theories, models and results to an urgent problem of socio-technological relevance (Klix, 1986).
There are, indeed, many publications on specific design problems presenting either experimental investigations (s. e. g. Card et al., 1983; Green, et al., 1983; Janda, 1984; Shackel, 1985; Borman and Curtis, 1985; Klix and Wandke, 1986, or catalogues of design recommendations (e. g. Spinas et al., 1982; DIN 66234/8, 1985).
Yet many questions cannot only be answered consulting those collections of experimental data or the guidelines derived from experimental research and experience. This may be due to the fact that many design questions are not wholly independent of the content of the information exchanged in human-computer interaction.
Questions of this kind include:

- What spatial arrangement should prompts be given on the screen?
- What are the best rules for abbreviating command names?
- Is the use of many but small menues preferable to that of a few but complex menues, or vice versa?

This list could easily be continued. It is interesting, however, that most of these questions have already been examined in experiments. But the problem remains of how to generalize the results obtained (Maguire, 1982).
One of the reasons for the difficulties arising when the results are being generalized might be that the answers to the questions do not primarily depend on well-investigated general laws of human information processing (e. g. "mechanisms" like perceptive grouping, formation of chunks, and memory scanning) but on the content (semantics) of the information that is to be processed.
The design of content aspects is made in many cases by system designers, implicitly without any consideration for human knowledge structures. A psychological approach can then only adapt the surface of the interface to the existing semantic structure of the system. It is supposed that the semantic structure of the system corresponds to the knowledge structure of the user.
The idea of starting with semantic system design was also put forward in Moran's (1981) Command Language Grammar.

```
-----------------------------------------------------------------------------
PKW-DATEN   FUNKTION  : AUSK   BEARBEITER: KUESPERT   MASKE: 26   HERSTELLER:
FORD   FAHRZEUGTYP: ESCORT   MODELL: L   HUBRAUM: 1263 CCM   LAENGE: 430 CM
DURCHSCHNVERBR.: 7,9 L   LEISTUNG: 40 KW   TANKINHALT: 45 L   AUSSTATTG.:
GRUND   HOECHSTGESCHW.: 164 KM/H   GLAS: GETOENT   POLSTER: NORMAL   LACK-
IERUNG: ROT   PREIS: 2-TUERIG:   BJ.82/11540 DM (100 %)   BJ.81/ 6960 DM
(60 %)   BJ.80/ 5900 DM (51 %)   BJ.79/ 5050 DM (44 %)   BJ.78/
4250 DM (37 %);   PREIS 4-TUERIG:   BJ.82/12130 DM (100 %)   BJ.81/ 7500
DM (62 %)   BJ.80/ 6500 DM (54 %)   BJ.79/ 5550 DM (46 %)   BJ.78/
4750 DM (39 %);   PREIS 5-TUERIG:   BJ.82/12690 DM (100 %)   BJ.81/ 8050 DM
(63 %)   BJ.80/ 7050 DM (56 %)   BJ.79/ 6100 DM (48 %)   BJ.78/ 5300 DM (42
%),   FOLGEMASKE: 37                              FOLGEFUNKTION: AUSK
-----------------------------------------------------------------------------
```

```
-----------------------------------------------------------------------------
PKW-DATEN                                    FUNKTION  : AUSK
MASKE: 25                                    BEARBEITER: KUESPERT
-----------------------------------------------------------------------------
HERSTELLER: OPEL          FAHRZEUGTYP: ASCONA          MODELL: BL
HUBRAUM: 1875 CCM         LAENGE: 433 CM         DURCHSCHNITTSVERBR.: 9,9 L
LEISTUNG:  55 KW    TANKINHALT:   60 L    AUSSTATTUNG: LUXUS    GLAS: NORMAL
POLSTER: BRAUN            HOECHSTGESCHW.: 157 KM/H         LACKIERUNG: BEIGE

PREIS 2-TUERIG: BJ.82/14415 DM (100 %)    BJ.81/ 9650 DM (67 %)

BJ.80/ 8250 DM (57 %)     BJ.79/ 7150 DM (50 %)     BJ.78/ 5950 DM (41 %)

PREIS 4-TUERIG: BJ.82/15025 DM (100 %)    BJ.81/10150 DM (68 %)

BJ.80/ 9250 DM (62 %)     BJ.79/ 7950 DM (53 %)     BJ.78/ 6550 DM (44 %)

PREIS 5-TUERIG: BJ.82/15645 DM (100 %)    BJ.81/10650 DM (68 %)

BJ.80/ 9250 DM (59 %)     BJ.79/ 7650 DM (50 %)     BJ.78/ 6300 DM (43 %)
-----------------------------------------------------------------------------
FOLGEMASKE: 43                                  FOLGEFUNKTION: AUSK
```

```
-----------------------------------------------------------------------------
PKW-DATEN                                    FUNKTION  : AUSK
MASKE: 18                                    BEARBEITER: KUESPERT
-----------------------------------------------------------------------------
HERSTELLER  : VW                   HUBRAUM          : 1588 CCM
FAHRZEUGTYP: PASSAT                LEISTUNG         :   55 KW
MODELL      : GL 5                 HOECHSTGESCHW.   :  164 KM/H
AUSSTATTUNG: GRUND                 TANKINHALT       :   45 L
LACKIERUNG  : GELBARZ              DURCHSCHNVERBR.  :  8,9 L
POLSTER     : NORMAL               LAENGE           :  443 CM
GLAS        : GETOENT

BAUJAHR      PREIS (2-TUERIG)      PREIS (4-TUERIG)      PREIS (5-TUERIG)
-------      ----------------      ----------------      ----------------
1982         15 290 DM  100 %      15 910 DM  100 %      16 325 DM  100 %
1981          9 400 DM   61 %       9 950 DM   63 %      10 300 DM   63 %
1980          8 350 DM   55 %       8 950 DM   56 %       9 150 DM   56 %
1979          7 200 DM   47 %       7 800 DM   49 %       7 750 DM   47 %
1978          6 300 DM   41 %       6 750 DM   42 %       6 650 DM   41 %
-----------------------------------------------------------------------------
FOLGEMASKE: 33                                  FOLGEFUNKTION: AUSK
```

Fig. 1. Three types of masks with different semantic-surface relations (from: Benz and Haubner, 1983)

The important role that the semantic structure of the interface plays can also be established in cases where it is considered only implicitly. Benz and Haubner (1983) demonstrated very nicely how the subjective load can be reduced and performance can be improved by surface structure adaptation. They did however stick to the "mechanisms" of information processing, when interpreting their results as effects of gestalt laws. Yet implicitly, they took into account the semantic structure of the information presented on the screen.

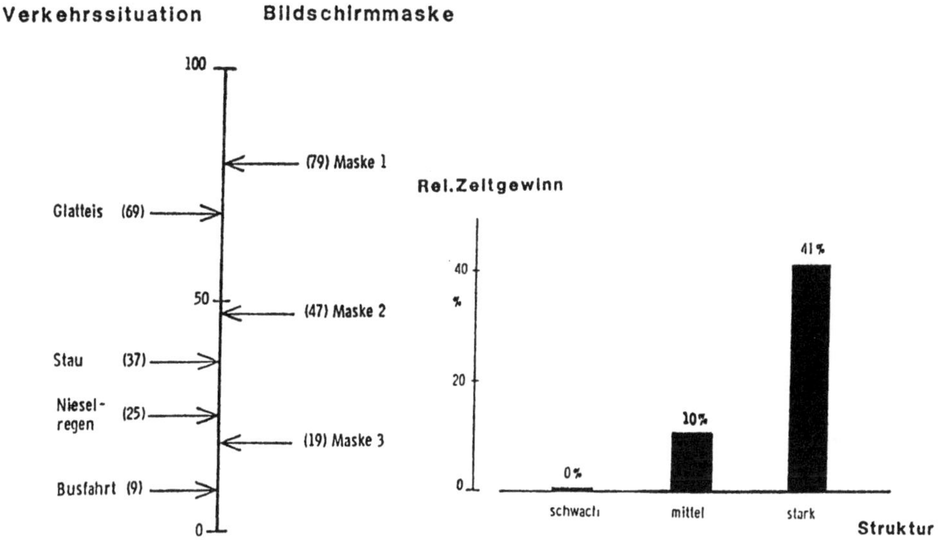

Erlebte Beanspruchung bei unterschiedlichen Bildschirmmasken im Vergleich zur erlebten Beanspruchung im Straßenverkehr

Leistungsverbesserung durch Strukturierung der Information

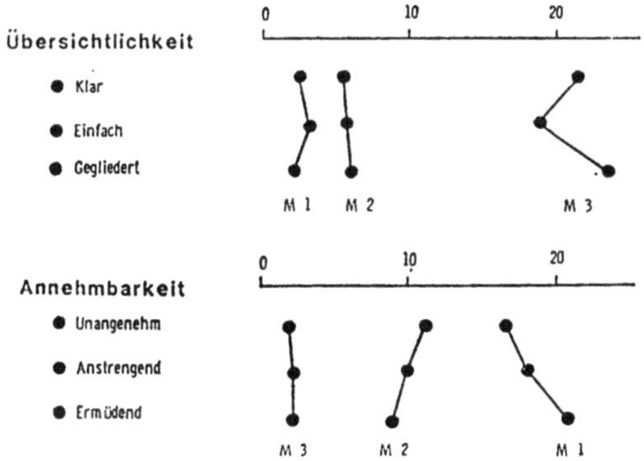

Zur subjektiven Bewertung der Bildschirmmasken

Quelle der Variation	Freiheitsgrade	Varianz	F_{test}	F_{krit} (ε=0.05)
Strukturen (S)	2	80.9	3.8	3.1
Test-personen (TP)	11	67.9	3.2	1.9
Wechsel-wirkung (S × TP)	22	9.2	0.4	1.7
Zellen (innerhalb)	72	21.5		

Varianzanalyse der Reaktionszeiten

Fig. 2. Experimental evaluation of the three different masks (from: Benz and Haubner, 1983)

Neglecting the semantic structure and only relying on the grouping mechanisms in perception, we would find that masks look similar, with the results differing very widely.

We suggest that the implicit consideration of the semantic structure should be made explicit.
In the example given by Benz and Haubner (1983), the problem is apparently trivial. But in many other cases it is not.
The first step in system design should therefore involve revealing the semantic structure of the information to be processed, i. e. analyzing the existing knowledge structure of future users in a certain domain. This is different from the procedures suggested by authors like Moran (1981), who proposed that system design should start from logical task analysis.
Logical task analysis reveals what a user *must* know before solving a task, rather than what he *does* know.
On the other hand, the analysis of existing knowledge (or the diagnosis of knowledge) is a problem that has not as yet been solved satisfactorily (s. Tergan, 1984).
In our experiments, we tried to tackle this problem by inducing certain semantic structure by means of instruction and experimental material.
In the first experiment, we sought to find out whether semantic aspects play any relevant role in interface design at all. And in the second experiment, we varied the semantic structure and tested the effects that this variation had on performance. The third one demonstrates the effects of compatibility between semantic and surface structure.

Exp. 1: Task-related versus complete presentation of data sets in system output

The starting point of this experiment was the question of how to present a set of data on the screen in a simple data correction task. Two alternatives were to be tested in particular:
- the presentation of whole data sets as screen masks with fixed positions for each item of the set; and
- the presentation of only the one item, which has to be changed by subjects; as a result different items will appear in one position on the screen.

A complete set of data – it was a simulated commercial order, with their total number forming a file of a fictitious sales management system – had the following structure in each case.

NUMBER OF THE ORDER: 142	DEGREE OF PRIORITY: 1
NAME OF THE CUSTOMER: VEB Carl Zeiss Jena	
POSTAL CODE: 6900	CITY: Jena
PRODUCT: [P]umpe	NUMBER OF ITEMS: 500
DATE OF DELIVERY: 85 05 10	MEANS OF TRANSPORT: DR

Fig. 3. Complete set of data of one order (example)

The task that subjects had to fulfill was to change one item of the orders (e. g. the date, the means of transport, or the number of items).
The psychological problem was: what is the semantic structure of this component of the interface, or, in other words, what kind of knowledge is activated by the task?

Subjects could interpret the task in two ways:

1. as to the change of a single item (independent of the order that the item forms part of; this is exactly the result of a logical task analysis; and
2. as to the change of an order resulting from the change of one characteristic of the order.

In the first case, no semantic structure was activated. The presentation was task-related only in a formal sense. In the second case, the change of one item was embedded in the semantic structure of the order.

Our hypothesis said that the choice of presentation modes depends on the spectrum of tasks to be solved in addition to the data correction task.

We therefore arranged three series of experiments with different additional tasks (s. fig. 4).

Third condition
Second condition
First condition

First task: change one item per order
(command = VERÄNDERN (142, 2)
Number of the order
Degree of priority

Subjects choose between:
Complete presentation of the data-set
Presentation of only the relevant item

Second task: add complete orders
(command = HINZUFÜGEN) – no parameters

No choice

Third task: check complete orders
(command ANZEIGEN (142))
Number of the order

No choice

Fig. 4. Tasks to be fulfilled in the three series of experiments

The first series only consisted of data correction tasks. In the second series subjects had to fulfill a second task: the input of data. A few complete orders were to be added to the file. In the third series, the third task was to check some of the orders stored. The first task – changing single items – was the same in all three conditions. Only when performing this task, could the subjects choose between displaying the complete data set and only displaying the item that was to be corrected.

The information displayed in the first case corresponded to figure 3. The information displayed in the second case is shown in figure 5.

PRODUCT: [P]umpe

Fig. 5. Example of information displayed when subjects chose the task-related structure (single item presentation)

The box indicates the position of the cursor. The results refer to the first task only.

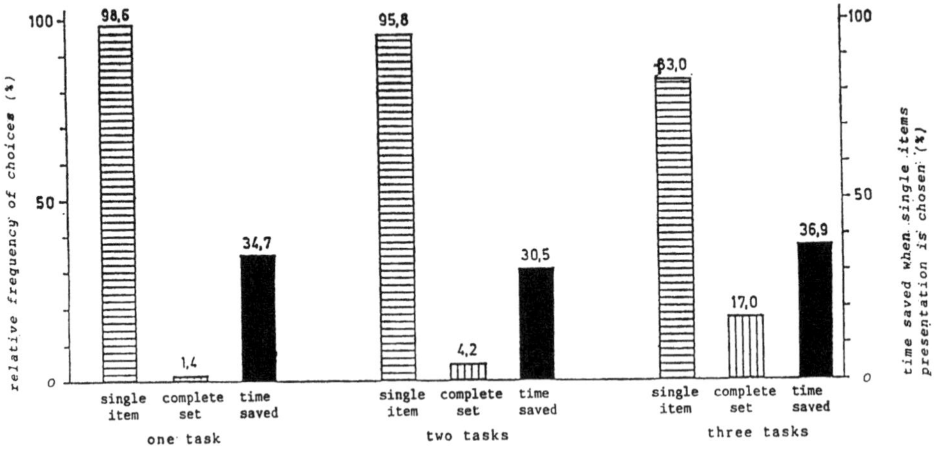

Fig. 6. Relative frequencies of choice of single item presentation and complete data set presentation with the time saved when single item presentation is chosen

Considering the frequency of choice, subjects prefered the task-related single item presentation in all three series.

Yet it is remarkable that, as the complexity of the task grew, subjects increasingly chose the presentation of complete data sets. As it is shown in figure 6, the choice of task-related presentation led to shorter times for command entry. Reductions required about one third of the time needed in the case of complete presentation in all three series.

This was certainly the reason why most subjects chose single item presentation.

It is therefore particularly interesting that, no matter what time was needed for command selection and keying, the relative frequency of the choice of semantically structured presentations increased as tasks became more complex.

Obviously, the subtask of making a "change" attained a new meaning when it was not fulfilled in isolation but in combination with other subtasks (data input and checking of orders.)

More subjects regarded the items to be changed as integrated parts of an order and chose the complete order for presentation on screen. All in all, it seems that the semantics of information does not only depend on the task that the subject is solving, but also on other tasks that might be solved with the help of the system.

The analysis of an isolated task is not sufficient for making design decisions. Since a complete analysis of all potential tasks is in many cases impossible, the analysis of the knowledge activated by the information displayed could serve as a basis for further designing.

Unfortunately, we could not really say what kind of knowledge was activated in our subjects when they were solving the change task in the three series of experiments.

We therefore relied on a second experiment, in which the task of the subjects was not changed, but the semantic structure of the experimental material was.

Exp. 2: Sequential versus simultaneous prompting

In this experiment, too, the problem was related to the interaction between the semantics of information and the mode of its presentation. The investigated component of the interface was system prompts, which guide the user when he is requested to enter data like parameters.

A frequent question in designing a system surface is whether a set of prompts should appear on the screen sequentially (i. e. that the second appears only when the first has been answered by the user) or simultaneously (i. e. all prompts relevant to a certain domain appear on the screen at the same time, and the action of the user consists in a kind of form-filling).

Our general hypothesis said again that answers to this design question depend on the meaning of the information prompted.

We assumed that simultaneous prompting techniques would prove more efficient only when there were semantic relations between concepts prompted. We therefore arranged for two systems: one prompted the user concerning the entry of data related to cooking recipes (the task was to program an automated cooking device); and the other prompted him concerning the entry of data relating to the construction of a house. Subjects were told that this would be necessary in order to give a well-founded estimate of the construction costs.

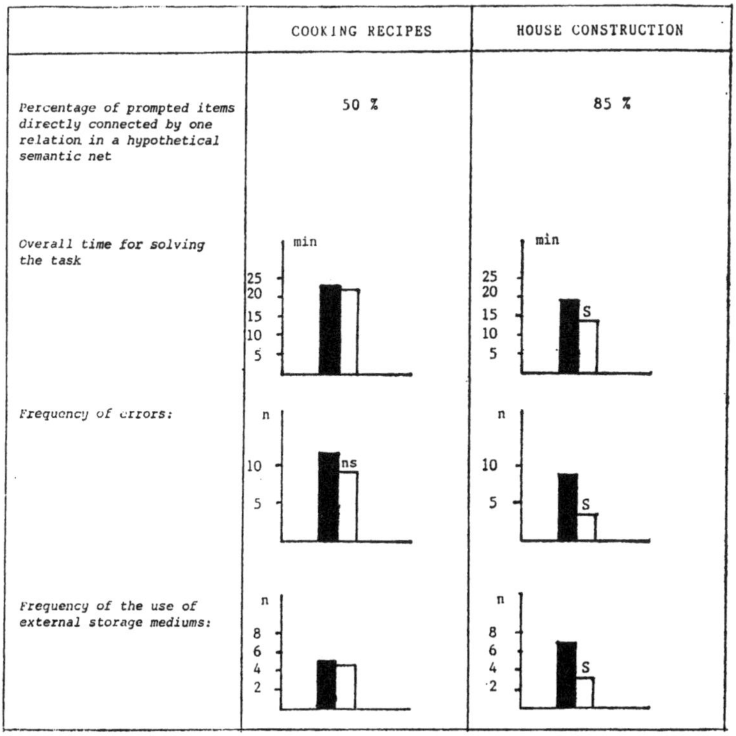

Fig. 7. Effects of sequential vs simultaneous prompting with different semantic structures

■ = sequential prompting

□ = simultaneous prompting

Both series were identical in terms of the number of prompts, the number of alternatives, the branches and all the other formal parameters. The important thing was, however, that they were different in terms of the semantic structure of information prompted – especially in the number of semantic relations between the concepts promted. In the case of the cooking recipes, only 50 % of all the concepts prompted were connected by a semantic relationship. Relations were analyzed with the help of the classification of semantic relations proposed by Klix in 1984. Such relations are e. g. sub-super concept relations, attribute relations, object relations, instrument relations etc. In the case of house construction, 85 % of the items prompted were semantically interrelated. Figure 7 shows a number of selected results.

The results show that significant improvements in dependent variables such as time, error and use of external storage mediums with simultaneous prompting were only made in the case of information with several semantic relations.

The consequence for the design process was that the shift from sequential to simultaneous prompting only became an advantage when there was a strong semantic coherence in the items prompted.

It may even be possible that in cases where the items prompted are not semantically related, the result will show quite the opposite trend: sequential prompting might prove better than simultaneous prompting. Yet this was not tested in our experiment.

Exp. 3: Verbally versus conceptually optimized abbreviations

While the investigated component of the interface in the last experiments was the system's output, it is in the third experiment the set of commands and their abbreviations.

The commands should be used in a programming environment.

The programmer could apply up to 75 different commands. Each command started a so-called technological action.

The denotations of the technological actions were used as original command names. In general the denotations consisted of several words and they were relatively long.

Since the future users of the system (the programmers) usually dislike to type long string sequences appropriate abbreviations should be found. Two different coding procedures were applied for this purpose (s. fig. 8).

---

aims of the 1st coding procedure (verbal level):

abbreviations should be
- as short as possible
- easy to speak (and verbally to rehearse)

aims of the 2nd coding procedure (conceptual level):

abbreviations should
- reflect the meaning of actions represented
- correspond to classes of actions (objects, processes, attributes)

Fig. 8. Two different procedures to abbreviate command names

The first procedure aimed at an optimal surface of the abbreviation – we call this the verbal level. The abbreviations should be short and have a smooth phonemic structure, i. e. they should be easy to speak. The meanings of the commands were not considered. The second procedure aimed at a correspondence between the meaning of the command and the surface (e. g.: different classes of concepts – objects, processes, and attributes – were clearly separated by hyphens).

The following table (tab. I) shows in five examples
- the original name of the action
- the abbreviation optimized on a verbal (or phonemic) level
- the abbreviation optimized on a conceptual (or semantic) level.

Tab. I. Examples for the two different abbreviation types

Original action name	Abbreviations	
	verbally optimized	conceptually optimized
Object code generation for module fram	OBFRA	OB – GEN – MF
Source code hierarchy checking	SOHIE	SO – CHE – H
Task builder control file preparation	TACON	TA – PRE – CF
Message file initializing	MEIN	ME – INI
Data base description for external level	DAEX	DA – GEN – EL

Each abbreviation code was to be learnt by a group of 8 subjects
The results look as follows (s. fig. 9).

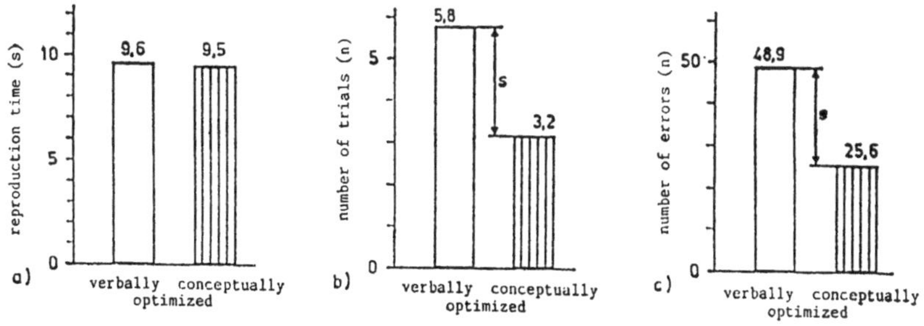

Fig. 9. Effect of two different forms of abbreviated command sets on
a) mean time for reproduction of abbreviations
b) mean number of repeated trials for fulfilling a learning criterion
c) mean of errors for all trials

In spite of a greater number of characters with the conceptually optimized code, there is no difference in time needed for the written reproduction. On the other hand, the number of trials and the mean error score dramatically decreased in the case of conceptually optimized abbreviations.

Although two remarks should be added at this point:
We expect that the differences disappear with a long period of training or use of the system.
Furthermore, this result is obviously only valid for large command sets.
But this does not impair the general statement that a design of command abbreviations which permits to recognize the meaning of a command facilitates tremendously the learning process.

Conclusion and critical evaluation of the approach

The three experiments demonstrated that the explicit consideration of semantic features of the interface (i. e. knowledge representation in the memory of the user) in the visible surface of the system can lead to improved performance.
But two points require a critical comment:
1. We did not really analyze the semantic structure. Instead, we derived hypothetic semantic structures from the experimental material on the assumption that subjects would develop the same structures.
2. It is very difficult to describe a semantic structure in detail. It is easy however to create such structures for several everyday objects or events like 'buy', 'teach', 'pay', 'give', or 'bird', 'fish', and 'tree'. These concepts are well-investigated by cognitive psychologists. Yet it is quite difficult to find semantic structures in processes of software development and use. The only exception is the domain of text editing – the psychologically best-known field of human-computer interaction.
How the problem of a missing analysis can be tackled should be demonstrated by an empirical study. Emphasis does not in this study lie on specific results, but on the method of obtaining the results.
If the decision has been taken to use a simultaneous prompting technique which is advantageous when the information prompted is semantically well-structured (as was shown in Exp. 2), then the problem will arise how the prompts should be arranged on the screen.
The same problem emerged in the design of a technological system for software development. But in contrast to cooking recipes or house construction, it was not possible to derive hypothetic semantic structures from it.
The only way was by revealing the really existing memory structures in programmers.
Here is a brief outline of the method – a card-sorting experiment.
97 prompts of 13 different technological actions were written down on small cards. The cards were to be sorted by 10 experienced programmers, who were instructed to arrange piles of cards of similar meanings. The number of cards in a pile and the total of all the piles were not considered in the instruction.

After sorting the cards into different piles, subjects were requested to arrange the cards of each pile in an order corresponding to the similarity of the prompts on the cards. The result of this procedure was a matrix. The cells of the matrix were filled by the frequencies with which the two kinds of prompts were sorted into the same pile.

Figure 10 shows a small section of such a matrix.

prompts

prompts	1	2	3	4	5	6	7	8	9	10	11	12	13
1	10		3										
2		10	4					3	3		4		
3			10		3						3		
4				10				3	4	4	7	5	6
5					10								
6						10	5					4	
7							10					4	
8								10	9	8	5	4	4
9									10	8	5	4	4
10										10	4	5	5
11											10	5	6
12												10	6
13													10

Fig. 10. Frequencies of sorting two prompts into the same pile

Only 13 prompts are presented. They are the 13 parameters necessary to start the technological section "assemble". Each number in the rows and columns represents a prompt. The number in the cells show how many of the ten subjects put two prompts into one pile.

This matrix, or the complete matrix of all prompts, was the starting point for a cluster analysis.

The results of the cluster analysis had to be carefully revised since a purely formal analysis would not have guaranteed a well-structured arrangement on the screen.

The revision could be supported by an analysis of the order of prompts within the piles. This information was not contained in the initial matrix.

In our example, we formed the following groups and arrangements of prompts (s. fig. 11).

1st group: Angabe von PSECT – Name gewünscht
Name der Daten – PSECT:
Name der Instructions – PSECT:

2nd group: Strukturblocktrace gewünscht:
Traceprotokoll gewünscht:
Crossreferenz gewünscht:

3rd group: Name des Quellmoduls:
Quellmodul wo gespeichert:
Ist Name ein TOP-Modul:

Single elements:
Ident.-Nr.
Form der Übersetzungsliste
Objektausgabe gewünscht
Objektmodul katalogisieren

Fig. 11. Groups of semantically similar prompts

Only after the arrangement of the groups in semantic terms did the design of the surface become relevant. In the next step, questions arose that were related to the "mechanisms" of human information processing.
A lot of possible surface structures may correspond to the one semantic structure (s. fig. 12 a–d).

Name des Quellmoduls:
Quellmodul wo gespeichert:
Ist Name ein TOP-Modul:

Ident.-Nr.:

Objektausgabe gewünscht:

Strukturblocktrace gewünscht:
Traceprotokoll gewünscht:
Crossreferenz gewünscht:

Angabe von PSECT-Name gewünscht:
Name der Daten-PSECT:
Name der Instruktions-PSECT:

Form der Übersetzungsliste:

Objektmodul katalogisieren:

Fig. 12a

Name des Quellmoduls: Quellmodul wo gespeichert: Ist Name ein TOP-Modul:

Ident-Nr.:

Objektausgabe gewünscht:

Strukturblocktrace gewünscht: Traceprotokoll gewünscht: Crossreferenz gewünscht:

Angabe von PSECT-Name gewünscht: Name der Daten-PSECT: Name der Instruktions-PSECT

Form der Übersetzungsliste:

Objektmodul katalogisieren:

Fig. 12b

Name des Quellmoduls:
Quellmodul wo gespeichert:
Ist Name ein TOP-Modul:

Ident.-Nr.

Objektausgabe gewünscht:

Strukturblocktrace gewünscht:
Traceprotokoll gewünscht:
Crossreferenz gewünscht:

Angabe von PSECT-Name gewünscht:
Name der Daten-PSECT:
Name der Instruktions-PSECT:

Form der Übersetzungsliste:

Objektmodul katalogisieren:

Fig. 12c

Name des Quellmoduls:
Quellmodul wo gespeichert:
Ist Name ein TOP-Modul:

Ident.-Nr:

Objektausgabe gewünscht:

Strukturblocktrace gewünscht:
Traceprotokoll gewünscht:
Crossreferenz gewünscht:

Angabe von PSECT-Name gewünscht:
Name der DATEN-PSECT:
Name der Instruktions-PSECT:

Form der Übersetzungsliste:

Objektmodul katalogisieren:

Fig. 12d

Fig. 12a–d. Different forms of surface structures (grouping) of identical semantic structure

These figures only indicate what design questions are to be dealt with after the layout of the semantic structure has been arranged.

In our opinion, the problem of how to have an adequate semantic structure reflected in the surface of the interface is very important in the cooperation between system designers and psychologists. In the same way as Card, Moran and Newell (1983) tried to provide the system designer with a catalogue of parameters of the "mechanisms" of human information processing, it ought to be possible to give him a number of methods enabling him to recognize the semantic structure of a knowledge domain before starting the system design.

As you can see, from our own investigations we are still at the beginning of this kind of cooperation, but we are convinced that this is the right way in which to continue psychological research into human-computer interface design.

References

Benz, C.; Haubner, P.: Gestaltung von Bildschirmmasken. In: Office Management. Suppl. (1983) 36–41.

Borman, L.; Curtis, B.: Human factors in computing systems – II, proceedings of the computer & human interaction conference (CHI' 85). Amsterdam: North Holland 1985.

Card, S. K.; Moran, T. P.; Newell, A.: The psychology of human-computer interaction. Hillsdale/NJ: Erlbaum 1983.

Green, T. R. G.; Payne, S. I.; van der Veer, G. C. (Eds.): The psychology of computer use. London: Academic Press .

Janda, A. (Eds.): Human factors in computing systems. Proceedings of the computer & human interaction conference (CHI' 83). Amsterdam: North Holland 1984.

Klix, F.: Über Wissensrepräsentation im menschlichen Gedächtnis. In: Gedächtnis, Wissen, Wissensnutzung. Eds.: Klix, F. Berlin: Deutscher Verlag der Wissenschaften 1984.

Klix, F.: MACINTER – Aim and goals. In: MACINTER I, proceedings of the 1st IUPsyS Network seminar on man-computer interaction research. Eds.: Klix, F.; Wandke, H. Amsterdam: North Holland 1986. S. 3–19.

Klix, F. (Ed.): Gedächtnis, Wissen, Wissensnutzung. Berlin: Deutscher Verlag der Wissenschaften 1984.

Klix, F.; Wandke, H. (Eds.): MACINTER I, proceedings of the first IUPsyS Network seminar on man-computer interaction research. Amsterdam: North Holland 1986.

Maguire, M.: An evaluation of published recommendations on the design of man-computer dialogues. Int. J. Man-Machine Studies 16 (1982) 237–261.

Moran, T. P.: Command Language Grammar: a representation for the user interface of interactive computer systems. Int. J. Man-Machine Studies 15 (1981) 3–50.

Shackel, B. (Ed.): Interact' 84, proceedings of the first IFIP conference on Human-Computer interaction. Amsterdam: North Holland 1985.

Spinas, P.; Troy, N.; Ulich, E.; Rohmert, E.: Leitfaden zur Einführung und Gestaltung von Arbeit mit Bildschirmarbeitssystemen. Rüschlikon: Gottlieb Duttweiler Institut 1982.

Tergan, S. O.: Diagnose von Wissensstrukturen. Deutsches Institut für Fernstudien an der Universität Tübingen. Forschungsbericht Nr. 30 (1984).

DIN 66234/8 (Entwurf) Bildschirmarbeitsplätze / Grundsätze der Dialoggestaltung. Berlin: Beuth Verlag 1985.

Author's adress:
Dr. H. Wandke
Sektion Psychologie der Humboldt-Universität
Oranienburger Str. 18, Berlin, DDR – 1020

From the IBM Science Center Heidelberg, FRG

Comparison of iconic and verbal editor commands: some results from scanning studies

By K. P. Muthig and G. Reinhardt

With 3 figures

Introduction

Rapid developments and improvements in computer technology during the last decades have led to an invasion of microcomputers into almost every working environment. Accordingly, most of those who use computer systems today are no data processing specialists but application specialists, who want to use computers as efficient tools within their respective application domains (e. g. banking, word processing, accounting). However, non-specialist users can interact with a computer system only via the interface of their respective application software. Thus, in order to make this interaction efficient, considerable attention has to be paid to the design of interfaces between the application software and the users.

Formerly, the interface has been widely neglected in data processing systems. Most of the users were system designers and developers themselves, and therefore, less emphasis was given to the interface than to the functionality and efficiency of the systems. However today, when millions of people use computer systems every day at their work, interfaces are required for casual, non-expert users which make the application system easy to learn, efficiently to use, and which support the understandability of such a system as perceived by its users. Accordingly, there is a growing interest in how the interface can be designed to accomodate the intended user (e. g. Moran, 1981; Sime and Coombs, 1983; Branscomb and Thomas, 1984).

One interesting aspect of current approaches to user oriented interface design is the emphasis on visual representation, and on the use of visualization techniques (e. g. windowing, pop-up menus, iconic representations) in order to improve man-computer interaction (Jervell and Olsen, 1985). This reflects the widely held assumption that the human mind is strongly visually oriented, and thus, people are able to acquire and to manipulate complex information more efficiently by means of graphical relationships in (complex) picture than by means of sequentially structured text (e. g. Raeder, 1985)

The use of icons at the interface to represent the objects within the filestore as well as the respective facilities available has been made popular by Xerox's STAR and Apple's LISA. Icons are graphical or pictorial signs which are related to their respective referents by means of a similarity relation which holds for a least one of their constituents (cf. Morris, 1938). Icons for both the STAR and the LISA interface were designed according to the desktop metaphor. That is, the icons remind the user of a desk together with the surrounding furniture and equipment to provide a suggestion of familiar objects and facilities in the user's office environment (e. g. documents, pens, wastepaper baskets).

In contrast to the conventional command driven interfaces, iconic interfaces to application systems seem to have some marked advantages, especially for the naive or casual user. Whereas a command driven interface requires a sound understanding of file store structure, as well as a high degree of expertise in its syntax and its semantics, syntax and semantics of iconic interfaces seem to be simple. An icon is referred to either by naming it, by locating its coordinates (mouse), or by pointing at it (cursor), and the semantics of the respective icon is defined by the operations that can be performed on this icon (Chang et al., 1985). In addition, due to the similarity relation existing between the sign and its referent, icons are thought to be understood solely on the basis of their visual characteristics, and to awake the same reaction in most people, irrespective of their background, education or nationality. Icons are also regarded to be visually more distinctive than a set of words, to allow for a more condensed information representation, and to be subjectively more appealing than text (e. g. Maguire, 1985; Raeder, 1985). Thus, since icons are thought to be easy to learn, easy to use, and by means of their iconicity, to provide the non-specialist user with a better chance to implicitely acquire a model of the application system structure, they are often regarded to represent the natural candidates for user oriented interfaces.

However, despite the attention which has been paid on visualization and iconic interfaces, only little is known on how to construct icons and iconic interfaces optimally. Questions like "What makes an icon a 'good' one?", "How are icons registered and processed in comparison to verbal commands?", and more generally, "When is it better to present information in form of icons than in form of verbal descriptions?" are mainly unresolved. Accordingly, there is no aggreement on standard icons in interface design, making cross-cultural or cross-linguistic use of them a problem (Korfhage and Korfhage, 1984). In general, the state of the art is defined by some commercial products and not by sound reasoning on empirical data.

Admittedly, there will be no simple answers to the forementioned questions, since there are many variants of (verbal) commands as well as of nonverbal symbols and icons. In addition, the choice between verbal and iconic commands may depend on the information to be presented, on the sophistication of the intended user, on the user's preference for pictorial or verbal information, and on the nature of the correspondence between the information to be presented and the information to be represented in the user's mental model. Thus, in order to reach some empirical criteria on which the use of verbal and iconic commands can be compared, experimental investigations have to be performed on standardized tasks to control for at least some of the influencing variables.

Some first steps in this direction have been undertaken recently at IBM Science Center Heidelberg (IBM HDSC), where an experimental text editing prototype has been developed in order to compare performance on iconic and verbal interfaces on standard editing tasks (cf. Keppel and Rohr, 1984). Since some of the results have been reported elsewhere (e. g. Rohr, 1984; Rohr and Keppel, 1985), only those aspects of this previous work will be summarized here which are of interest for the present study.

Since the prototype editor was designed to allow for comparison of verbal and iconic command sets, the characteristics of its interface are easily changable without altering the overall system structure. For instance, the surface of all command fields can be deliberately changed from command words to icons, thus allowing for an integration of any new set of icons or command words. The basic structure of the interface to the prototype software system models a two-state editor. The "file handling" state is characterized by commands which control for sequentially structured events involving complete documents (e. g. "print", "select", "store"). The "editing" state is characterized by commands which control for spatial manipulative operations within a selected document (e. g. "insert word", "delete line"). There were the same number of commands associated with both states.

According to different design principles, three icon sets (FUNC, NOFUNC, OBJECTS) were developed depicting the system commands under investigation (see fig. 1 for an example). In addition, a conventional verbal command set (VERBAL) has been run on the experimental prototype editor.

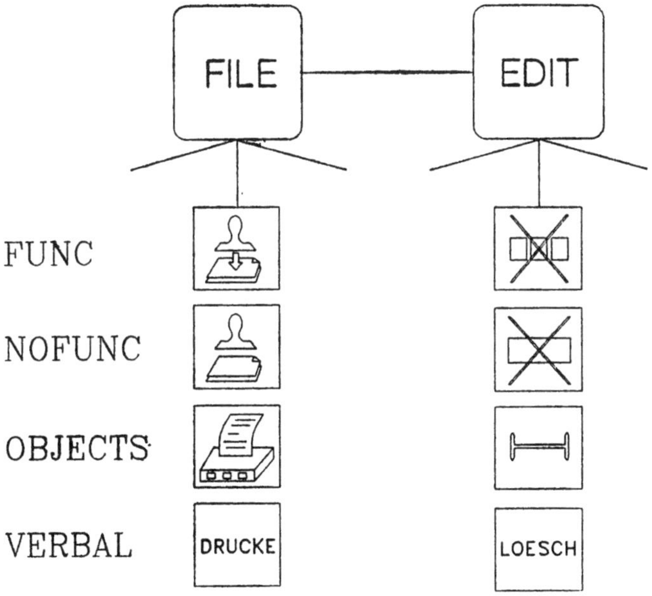

Fig. 1. Examples for the commands used on the experimental prototype editor

FUNC (functional) and NOFUNC (nonfunctional) icons were constructed according to the results of preliminary studies (cf. Rohr and Keppel, 1984) by combining those features from selected sets (e. g. rectangles, abstract symbols, numbers, letters, pictorial symbols) which carried the most salient meaning elements with respect to required command function. In general, file handling commands were better represented via pictorial symbols and rectangles, whereas editing commands were better represented via abstract symbols and letters. FUNC icons differed from NOFUNC icons however with respect to the presence of functional or manipulative cues within each icon. FUNC icons associated with the "file handling" state contained arrows as additional (functional) cues to make the action component more salient, whereas, for FUNC icons associated with the "editing" state, those elements of the icons were marked which were relevant for the required cursor actions. Accordingly, NOFUNC icons contained neither functional elements nor any marking of elements to support cursor actions. Elements of the third set of icons used (OBJECTS) were constructed in close correspondence to the desktop metaphor. Accordingly, these icons resembled more concrete objects (e. g. documents, pens, wastepaper baskets). In the command set VERBAL, however, all icons were replaced by their corresponding verbal command words.

FUNC and NOFUNC icon sets were tested with respect to performance (time, errors) and number of help requests at the prototype editor during usual editing tasks. These experiments revealed differences between iconic and verbal command sets with respect to the number of help requests during the tasks, as well as differences between FUNC and NOFUNC icons as a function of familiarity or training with the respective sets (e. g. Rohr, 1984; Rohr and Keppel, 1984). All in all, the results of these previous studies suggest that there may be processing differences in response to iconic and verbal command sets as well as processing differences with respect to the kind of operations to be performed (file handling, editing). However, since these experiments were designed to investigate ease of learning and quality of performance of different command sets on usual editing tasks, their results provide no straightforward explanation of what may be responsible for the observed differences (e. g. item complexity, task differences).

In order to get further insights into the characteristics of the iconic and verbal command sets used, processing of these command sets was analyzed in more detail in the present study. Since little is known on this material, we started by investigating how the respective commands may be encoded in shortterm memory, and how they will be retrieved from there. Since the commands used are highly idiosyncratic and probably possess characteristics that affect the process under investigation, we decided to adopt a well studied paradigm in cognitive psychology. This was to garanty that there are reliable data available by which the interpretation of the results can be guided.

One of the most prominent paradigms for investigating search and comparison processes in short-term (episodic) memory is the item recognition paradigm (e. g. Sternberg, 1966, 1969 a, b). In this paradigm, subjects are required to memorize a short list (the memory list) of sequentially presented items on each trial. After a brief delay, a single item (the test stimulus) is presented and a speeded yes/no decision is required whether the test stimulus is a member of the memory list (positive trial) or not (negative trial). Reaction time (RT) is measured from the onset of the test stimulus to the occurrence of the response. Typically, mean RTs on both positive and negative trials increase linearily as memory list size increases with the slopes of both RT functions being approximately equal. Although other interpretations are possible, the original, and most elegant account of this finding is that search through the items in short-term memory (the memory set) is serial and exhaustive, and not self-terminating as common sense may suggest (e. g. Sternberg, 1966, 1969 a, b, 1975; Wescourt and Atkinson, 1976; McNicol and Stuart, 1980).

Since Sternberg (1966) introduced the item recognition paradigm, the basic results have been replicated with surprising accuracy, at least for simple or well learned materials (e. g. digits, letters, words). However, some empirical evidence has been found for the notion that parallel processing may be the mode of retrieval when the item recognition paradigm is applied to pictures, or when verbal items have a high imagery value (e. g. Paivio, 1971; Seamon, 1972; De Rosa and Tkacz, 1976; Kerst, 1976). At least, this seems to be true when the probe is processed by the right hemisphere (e. g. Bersted, 1983).

Since the command sets run in previous experiments are either verbal (VERBAL) or iconic (FUNC, NOFUNC, OBJECTS), results obtained in the item recognition paradigm should reflect these differences. Since the iconic command sets also seem to differ in concreteness (OBJECTS vs. FUNC or NOFUNC), which has been proven to be an important variable for processing, and to be independent of imagery (e. g. Day and Bellezza, 1983), the respective RT functions should reflect these differences, too. Whether the addition of functional elements FUNC vs. NOFUNC) will have an effect within the item recognition paradigm is as open to question as whether the commands associated with the file handling state will be differently processed from those associated with the editing state.

Method

Subjects

Twenty-eight students and staff members at IBM Sciene Center Heidelberg participated in the experiment. The subjects were randomly assigned to one of four groups corresponding to the four command sets used.

Materials

Three icon sets (FUNC, NOFUNC, OBJECTS) and one verbal command set (VERBAL) were used in this experiment (s. fig. 1 for an example). Each of the four command sets had been run in previous experiments on the experimental text editing prototype at IBM HDSC. Each set contained 16 commands: eight commands for file handling, and eight commands for text editing.

Memory list items

For each command set, memory lists of sizes S (S = 2, 4, 6) were constructed from the eight commands within the file handling and the editing subset, respectively. The commands were randomly assigned to memory lists and not repeated within a memory list.

Procedure

The subjects were required to memorize lists of 2, 4, or 6 sequentially presented items on each trial. After the last memory list item had been presented, an end-of-list marker appeared on the screen. Thereafter, the test stimulus was displayed until the subjects had responded. The subjects were required to make a speeded yes/no decision whether the test stimulus was a member of the memorized list or not.

At the beginning of each trial, a fixation dot marked the center of the viewing area and served as a cue to start the next trial. Pushing the space bar on the keyboard removed the fixation dot from the screen. Thereafter, the memory list items were presented sequentially for 900 msec each, with an interstimulus intervall of 300 msec. Nine hundred milliseconds after the last memory list item, an end-of-list marker was displayed for 900 msec. One second later, the test stimulus appeared and remained on the screen until the subjects had responded. Thereafter, the fixation dot reappeared on the screen and the next trial started.

Subjects were encouraged to respond quickly and to keep error rates low. Item recognition errors were fed back by an "ERROR" cue, flickering on the screen. RTs longer than 1.6 sec were reported back by displaying "FASTER RESPONDING REQUIRED" on the screen. All trials on which either an item recognition error or a response longer than 1.6 sec occured were repeated within the remaining trials.

Design

The experiment based on a 2 (trial type: positive vs negative) x 3 (list size: 2, 4, 6) x 2 (command type: file handling vs editing) x 4 (command set: FUNC, NOFUNC, OBJECTS, VERBAL) factorial design. Command set was a between-subjects factor, all other experimental manipulations were within subjects. Thus, each subject was run in the file handling and in the editing condition for one of the four command sets. The sequence of the file handling and editing condition was counterbalanced across subjects.

Subjects were tested individually. Within each of the two 40-min successive sessions, each subject had to complete 30 training trials and 120 correct experimental trials. Between sessions there was a 10 min pause.

Equipment

The experiments were controlled by an IBM PC-XT. Memory list items and test stimuli were presented on an IBM Color Display next to the PC monitor. Viewing distance was approximately 70 cm. The subjects had to indicate their yes/no decisions via the PC-keyboard. Trials were initiated via the space bar of the keyboard whereas the adjacent keys DEL and INS indicated the YES or NO decision, respectively.

Results and Discussion

In order to prevent for carry-over effects and to keep the number of subjects at a moderate size, subjects had to be nested under command sets. However, this implies that the power of the F-Test with respect to a possible command set effect is smaller than for any other effect. In order to identify possible differences in the processing of different command sets it is therefore more promising to analyze the data for each command set group separately.

RTs were discarded for trials in which an error was made or the time itself exceeded 1.6 sec. Since the proportion of time errors was small (less than 1.8 % of all responses), only item recognition errors were subjected to an error analysis.

Thus, for each group item recognition errors and RTs from correct trials were analyzed with respect to a 2 (trial type: positive, negative) x 3 (list size: 2, 4, 6) x 2 (command type: editing, file handling) factorial design (all factors beeing within-subjects factors).

VERBAL set

Results for this command class are presented first because they can serve as a base line (memory scanning for words) against which all other results (memory scanning for icons) can be compared.

Recognition error rates across conditions ranged from 1.4 % to 19.1 %, averaging 7.6 % (s. fig. 2).

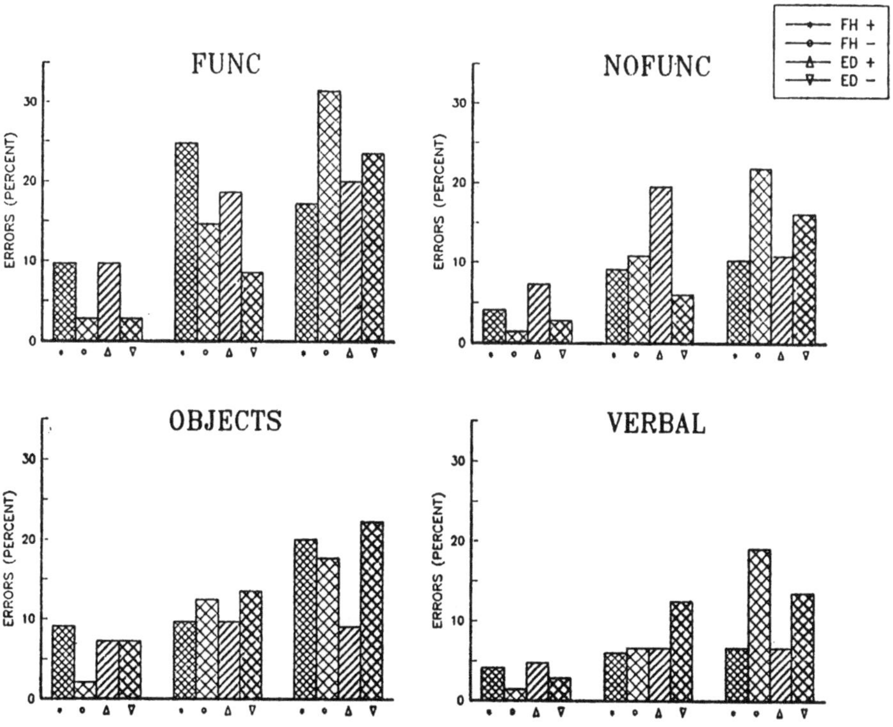

Fig. 2. Item recognition errors within command sets as a function of trial type, list size, and command type

In general, more errors were made with increasing list size, $F\ (2,12) = 5.17$, $MSe = 5.42$, $p < .05$, but errors increased differently on positive and negative trials, $F\ (2,12) = 4.41$, $MSe = 3.59$, $p < .05$. Post hoc comparisons (Scheffé tests) revealed that error means significantly increased with list size on negative trials, but that there was only a slight (nonsignificant) increase on positive trials. Although the error rates on positive and negative trials did not differ significantly, the respective differences grew with increasing list size.

The relationship between RT performance and list size for each combination of command type and trial type is depicted in figure 3. Standard errors of the means ranged from 11 to 22 msec, and averaged 18.2 msec.

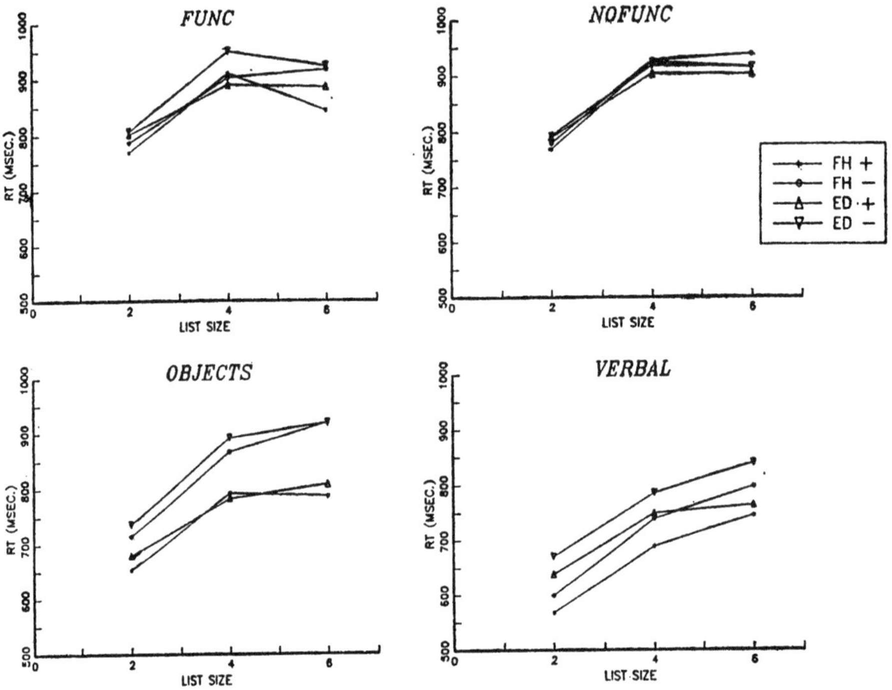

Fig. 3. Mean correct RTs within command sets as a function of trial type, list size, and command type

Analysis of variance revealed that RTs were longer for "NO" than for "YES" decisions, $F\ (1,6) = 27.03$, $MSe = 33077.74$, $p < .01$, and that RTs increased with list size, $F\ (2,12) = 47.66$, $MSe = 87547.83$, $p < .01$. There was also a significant list size x command type interaction, $F\ (2,12) = 4.33$, $MSe = 13508.90$, $p < .05$.

Analysis of this interaction effect revealed that in the file handling condition RTs significantly increased with each increase in list size, whereas in the editing condition the increase from $S = 4$ to $S = 6$ was not significant. Since RTs in response to file handling commands tended to be smaller than in response to editing commands, the significant difference observed at $S = 2$ diminished for larger list sizes.

Mean RTs show linear list size effects. Linear regression accounted for about 95 % of the variance in all but one of the RT functions. The only condition in which the data are not so closely fit by a linear function is the positive editing ($R^2 = 83.7$). The reason why there is a departure from linearity in the positive editing condition remains unclear. At least there ist no indication that this comes about because of unusual large variance in the respective cells. Whether this departure from linearity can be replicated has to be shown in further experiments.

With the exception of the non-linear function for the positive editing condition the RT results are similar to the results usually obtained with the item recognition paradigm. However, item recognition errors are relatively high (especially on negative trials for $S > 2$) compared to those usually reported when word material has been used. However, since the command words used in this study (e. g. "replace", "delete", "select") are neither as overlearned nor as concrete as the familiar nouns typically used in these studies (e. g. names, vegetable), they are also harder to memorize. Taking this into account, the obtained error results are plausible.

OBJECTS set

Item recognition errors ranged from 2.1 % to 22.2 %, averaging 10.2 % (s. fig. 2). Error rates increased with list size, $F(2,12) = 12.43$, MSe = 4.64, $p < .01$. There is also an indication of a trial type x command type interaction, though this interaction just failed to reach statistical significance, $F(1,6) = 4.98$, MSe = 4.63, $p = .07$. Inspection of this interaction revealed that more errors were made for file handling than for editing commands on positive trials, whereas on negative trials the reverse was true. However, only for editing commands more errors were made on negative than on positive trials, whereas for file handling commands there was no such difference.

The mean correct RTs are shown in figure 3. Standard errors of the means ranged from 16.4 to 20.3 msec, averaging 19.6 msec.

Analysis of variance for the RT data revealed that RTs were longer on negative trials than on positive trials, $F(1,6) = 39.55$, MSe = 87017.74, $p < .01$, and that RTs increased with list size, $F(2,12) = 47.56$, MSe = 89211.13, $p < .01$. However there was also a significant interaction between trial type and list size, $F(2,12) = 5.01$, MSe = 27876.25, $p < .05$. Thus, RTs not only were longer on negative trials than on positive trials but the RT differences increased with list size. On the other hand, RTs for list sizes $S = 4$ and $S = 6$ did not differ significantly from each other for both positive and negative trials. However, both were significantly longer than mean RT for $S = 2$.

Mean RTs show less pronounced linear list size effects due to the nonsignificant increases in RT for list sizes $S = 6$. The best fit was obtained for the file handling negative condition ($R^2 = 92.7$), the worst for the file handling positive condition ($R^2 = 71.99$).

In general, more errors were made in response to OBJECT commands than in response to VERBAL commands. However, the error pattern is difficult to explain since there are marked differences between single icons in the file handling condition as well as in the editing condition. For instance, errors at S = 2 in positive file handling, and at S = 4 in negative file handling were almost completely due to errors made in response to the "edit" icon. In order to get further hints on possible reasons for the obtained differences in this susceptibility to errors single items analyses have to be performed. However, these are beyond the scope of the present paper.

The most interesting result for this command set is the difference in RT for positive and negative trials, which increases with list size. This kind of difference in RT functions is usually obtained when search in short-term memory is at least partially selective (e. g. Naus, 1974; Ulrich and Muthig, 1983; Muthig and Ulrich, 1985). This indicates that there may be a partition for the representation of OBJECT icons in memory which can be selectively entered in the comparison process. This in turn implies that OBJECT icons can be categorized with respect to global or local features. In fact, OBJECT icons seem to differ in at least two characteristics: Some icons possess global Gestalt characteristics (concrete objects) whereas others are more abstract and/or more visually complex.

NOFUNC set

Recognition error rates within this command set ranged from 1.4 % to 21.8 %, averaging 10 % (see figure 2). List size significantly affected the number of errors made, $F(2,12) = 6.11$, MSe = 8.76, $p < .05$, but its influence differed for positive and negative trials, $F(2,12) = 4.47$, MSe = 6.76, $p < .05$. On negative trials, errors rates monotonely increased with list size, on positive trials, however, the error rate at S = 4 was higher than the error rate at S = 6 which in turn was higher than the rate at S = 2. Error rates between positive and negative trials did not differ for S = 2. For S = 4 more errors were made on positive trials whereas for S = 6 more errors were made on negative trials.

Again, the icons were not equal susceptible to errors. For instance, the NOFUNC icon "rename" was responsible for more than half of all errors made on negative trials in the file handling condition. On the other hand, the icon "delete" accounted for almost every error made in the editing condition at S = 6. Again, this error pattern can only be resolved by forthcoming single item analysis.

The relevant RT data are shown in figure 3. Standard errors of the means ranged from 17.1 to 24.2 msec averaging 22.7 msec.

Analysis of variance revealed a significant list size effect on RTs, $F(2,12) = 38.23$, MSe = 89644.28, $p < .01$. This effect was produced by significantly shorter RTs for S = 2 than for S = 4 and S = 6 which in turn did not differ.

Linear list size effects are therefore poor: With the exception of the negative file handling condition ($R^2 = 80.2$) linear regression accounted for only about 72 % of the variance for all other conditions. In contrast to both VERBAL and OBJECTS command sets, there was neither an effect of command class nor of trial type on RT for NOFUNC icons. The most interesting result for this icon group is, that there is no difference in RT between S = 4 and S = 6. This may be due to either shorter RTs at S = 6 or longer RTs at S = 4. There are at least the following explanations for this result. Since there are only eight commands for both the file handling and the editing subset, the test stimulus may become predictable for S= 6. This implies, that at least in a portion of trials the test stimulus can be responded to by not searching through the memory set, but by searching through the complementary set. In addition there is a higher probability that memory lists of size S = 6 contain icons which are visually similar (e. g. "scroll up" and "scroll down", "save" and "select"). Because of their similarity, these icons may form a separate category in short-term memory which can be searched selectively in the comparison process in a portion of trials (cf. Muthig und Ulrich, 1985). This also would produce shorter RTs at S = 6. On the other hand, with a reference set of eight commands, presenting four commands produces the maximum of uncertainty with respect to the response decision, since at S = 4 neither memorizing the complementary set nor categorizing similar icons will pay off. This in turn would explain why RTs at S = 4 are higher than to be expected.

FUNC set

Recognition error rates across conditions ranged from 2.8 % to 31.3 %, averaging 15.3 % (s. fig. 2). Analysis of variance revealed a significant effect of list size on the number of errors made, $F\,(2,12) = 8{,}12$, MSe = 19.61, $p < .01$. There was also an indication of a trial type x list size interaction though the interaction effect just failed to reach statistical significance, $F\,(2,12) = 3.33$, MSe = 20.8, $p = .07$. Inspection of the error data revealed that mean errors progressively increased with list size on negative trials, whereas on positive trials more errors where made at S = 4 than at S = 2, with the error rate at S = 6 at an intermediate level. For S = 6, more errors were made on negative than on positive trials, whereas for S < 6 more errors were made on positive than on negative trials.

Again, there is no simple explanation for the obtained error pattern, since some of the icons used were more prone to errors than others. As for the NOFUNC commands, it was the icon "delete" which accounted for most errors in the editing condition at S = 6. In the file handling condition very high error rates were obtained for the icons "save", "show", "send", and "rename". Since error rates in response to FUNC icons not only are extremely high but also due to the effect of specific icons, data have to be analyzed on single icon level in order to reach a sound explanation.

The relevant RT data for functional icons are shown in figure 3. Standard errors of the means ranged from 17.9 to 22.5 msec, averaging 21.7 msec.

Analysis of variance revealed an effect of list size on RTs, $F\,(2,12) = 15.66$, MSe = 149699.21, $p < .01$. There was also an indication for a trial type x list size interaction, though the interaction effect did not reach statistical significance, $F\,(2,12) = 3.58$, MSe = 19803, $p = .06$. However, this interaction was qualified by a significant three factor interaction between trial type, list size, and command type, $F\,(2,12) = 3.80$, MSe = 27096.39, $p < .05$. As for NOFUNC commands, RTs were significantly shorter at S = 2 than at S = 4 or at S = 6. However, this time RTs at S = 4 in the negative editing condition were higher than in any condition, whereas RTs at S = 6 in the positive file handling condition were shorter than in any other condition at S = 6 or even at S = 4. Accordingly, linear list size effects are considerably small this time. Less than 50 % of the respective variances were accounted for by linear regression.

If there had not been these marked differences at S = 4 and S = 6, the overall pattern of RTs had been similar to that for NOFUNC icons. However, the present data indicate that the addition of functional elements (arrows) as well as the marking of elements within the icons of this command set clearly have an effect on RT, at least in some conditions and/or for some of the icons. Thus icons within the FUNC command set seem not to be homogenous. In general, however, the obtained data are consistent with the interpretation given for NOFUNC icons.

Conclusion

If one puts the results for the four command sets together, some interesting aspects can be noted. First, the error rates obtained for all command sets are higher than what is usually reported from scanning experiments. The higher error rates for the VERBAL set in comparison to common nouns may reflect that verbal commands (at least those used here) are more difficult to remember. A more detailed analysis for elements of the VERBAL set may provide hints as to where there should be an increase in command mnemonics. Concerning the error rates made in response to the iconic command sets single item analyses are urgent. Error rates are not only very high, but are due to specific icons. In general, the increase in error rates from OBJECTS via NOFUNC to FUNC can be interpreted as a decrease in overall concreteness (OBJECTS vs. NOFUNC, FUNC) accompanied by an increase of visual complexity. This is especially true for the difference between NOFUNC and FUNC, since both command sets only differ in the presence of additional (functional) elements.

With respect to the RT data there are marked differences between VERBAL, OBJECTS and both NOFUNC and FUNC RT functions. Whereas RT functions for the VERBAL set show strong linear list size effects, comparable effects are not obtained for the iconic command sets. Whether this is due to general "pop out" effects for icons possessing global Gestalt characteristics or to some kind of parallel processing can not be decided on the present data. The RT functions for the OBJECTS set indicate a kind of self terminating search process. It has been argued that this may be due to a categorization of this icon set in more concrete/pictorial and more abstract/iconic icons. Whether there is evidence for this hypothesis has to be shown in further experiments, where these features of the icons are systematically varied. RT data for NOFUNC icons differ from both VERBAL and OBJECTS data. The only variation in RT functions is due to the increase in list size from S = 2 to S = 4. Whether for NOFUNC icons the relatively small stimulus ensemble (eight commands) is responsible for this effect, since it can be further reduced by clustering of visual similar icons, has to be tested using enlarged stimulus sets. Similar arguments can be started for the FUNC RT data. However, the increase in local complexity due to the addition of the functional elements with respect to the NOFUNC icons, is directly reflected in less homogeneous RT functions. Since this effect is only obtained in some conditions, this indicates that some icons have been made more salient than others. If this is true, then the interpretation given for NOFUNC data holds also for FUNC data.

Anyway, detailed item analyses have to be performed for all command sets in order to identify icons or commands which differ either in RT or in error rates from their respective means. However, the results of the present experiment show that the item recognition paradigm is sensitive for command sets being constructed according to different principles. Although the present study was nothing but a first start, it was successful in giving at least hints as to where processing differences for iconic and verbal commands can be located. Thus, the item recognition paradigm can be regarded as a valuable method to perform a more detailed analyses of commands, actually used on current systems.

References

Bersted, C. T.: Memory scanning of described images and undescribed images: Hemispheric differences. Mem. Cognit. 11 (1983) 129–136.

Branscomb, L. M.; Thomas, J. C.: Ease of use: a system design challenge. IBM Systems J. 23 (1984) 224–235.

Chang, S. K.; Jungert, S.; Levialdi, S.; Tortora, G.; Ichikawa, T.: An image processing language with icon-assisted navigation. IEEE Transactions on Software Engineering. SE-11 (1985) 811–819.

Day, J. C.; Bellezza, F. S.: The relation between visual imagery mediators and recall. Mem. Cognit. 11 (1983) 251–257.

DeRosa, D. V.; Tkacz, S.: Memory scanning of organized visual material. J. Exp. Psychol.: Hum. Lear. Mem. 2 (1976) 688–694.

Jervell, H. R.; Olsen, K. A.: Icons in man-machine communications. Behaviour and Information Technology. 3 (1985) 249–254.

Keppel, E.; Rohr, G.: Prototyping – a method to explore human factor aspects in application software. In: Human factors in organizational design and management. Eds.: Hendrick, H. W.; Brown, W. Amsterdam: North Holland 1984.

Kerst, S. M.: Interactive visual imagery and memory search for word and pictures. Mem. Cognit. 4 (1976) 573–580.

Korfhage, R. R.; Korfhage, M. A.: The nature of visual languages. Proceedings of the 1984 IEEE Workshop on Visual Languages. Hiroshima: December 1984. P. 177–183.

Maguire, M. C.: A review of human factors guidelines and techniques for the design of graphical human-computer interfaces. Comput. Graph. 9 (1985) 221–235.

McNicol, D.; Stuart, G. W.: Reaction time and the study of memory. In: Reaction Times. Ed.: Welford, A. T. London: Academic Press 1980.

Moran, T. P.: The command language grammar: a representation for the user interface of interactive computer systems. International J. of Man-Machine Studies 15 (1981) 3–50.

Morris, Ch. W.: Foundations of the theory of signs. Chicago: University of Chicago Press 1938.

Muthig, K. P.; Ulrich, R.: Selective search in short-term memory under ideal conditions of test-stimulus categorization. Mem. Cognit. 13 (1985) 29–36.

Naus, M. J.: Memory search of categorized lists: a consideration of alternative self-terminating search strategies. J. Exp. Psychol. 102 (1974) 992–1000.

Paivio, A.: Imagery and verbal processes. New York: Holt, Rinehart & Winston 1971.

Raeder, G.: A survey of current graphical programming techniques. IEEE Comput. 18 (1985) 11–25.

Rohr, G.: Understanding visual symbols. Proceedings of the 1984 IEEE Workshop on Visual Languages. (pp. 184–191). Hiroshima: 1984. P. 184–191.
Rohr, G.; Keppel, E.: Zur begrifflichen und bildlichen Kodierung von Operationsfolgen bei der Mensch-Computer-Interaktion. Z. Psychol. 193 (1985) 377–384.
Seamon, J. G.: Imagery codes and human information retrieval. J. Exp. Psychol. 96 (1972) 468–470.
Sime, M. E.; Coombs, M. J. (Eds.): Designing for human-computer communication. London: Academic Press 1983.
Sternberg, S.: High-speed scanning in human memory. Science 153 (1966) 652–654.
Sternberg, S.: Memory-scanning: mental processes revealed by reaction-time experiments. Am. Sci. 57 (1969a) 421–457.
Sternberg, S.: The discovery of processing stages: Extensions of Donder's method. In: Attention and Performance. Vol. II. Ed.: Koster, W. G. Amsterdam: North Holland 1969b.
Sternberg, S.: Memory scanning: New findings and current controversies. Quart. J. Exp. Psychol. 27 (1975) 1–32.
Ulrich, R.; Muthig, K. P.: Darbietungsabhängige Vergleichsprozesse bei kategorial zerlegbaren Gedächtnismengen. Z. exp. angew. Psychol. 30 (1983) 673–694.
Wescourt, K. T.; Atkinson, R. C.: Fact retrieval processes in human memory. In: Handbook of Learning and Cognitive Processes. Vol. 4. Ed.: Estes, W. K. Hillsdale: Erlbaum 1976.

Author's address:
Dr. K.-P. Muthig
Psychologisches Institut der Universität Tübingen
Friedrichstr. 21, D – 7400 Tübingen

From the Department of Psychology, Technical University of Darmstadt, FRG

On the usability of verbal and iconic command representations

By J. Wandmacher and U. Müller

With 4 figures

Introduction

The purpose of the present study was to compare the usability of verbal and iconic representations of commands in human-computer interaction. Usability is defined here by the speed and accuracy of performance in menu selection and recognition of command representations. Of course, this very limited meaning of usability is not sufficient for a comprehensive evaluation of verbal and iconic command representations with respect to ease of use and learnability of interface languages. Furthermore, shorter response times and greater accuracy to either verbal or iconic command representations will not be crucial for the current debate about direct manipulation interfaces (Shneiderman, 1983; Hutchins, Hollan and Norman, 1986), since direct manipulation interfaces can be realized both with verbal and iconic command representations.

Nevertheless, an experimental comparison of performance with verbal and iconic command representations seems to be important for two reasons. First, for the purpose of optimizing performance in human-computer interaction it is necessary to know whether verbal or iconic command representations can be faster selected and responded to. In a similar vein, various devices for cursor positioning have been compared (e. g., Card, Moran and Newell, 1983; section 7.2). Second, differences in response time and accuracy to verbal and iconic command representations could indicate characteristics of human information processing which are relevant to human-computer interaction.

Relevant experimental results. Recognition of words and icons has been compared in several experiments. The time to read a word is faster than the time to name an object or a figure (Cattell, 1885). Nonverbal reaction time to figures is, however, sometimes faster than to words (Kolers, 1969). For example, in a nonverbal reaction task, Fraisse (1968) found a small but significant advantage of the line drawings of fifteen concrete objects over the names of these objects (245 vs. 259 ms). The subjects responded with a key when they had identified the stimulus. Following this response the stimulus disappeared and the subjects had to name the stimulus. In a threshold experiment using the same line drawings and words Fraisse obtained mean threshold durations of 21.7 and 24.7 ms for the line drawings and words, respectively, yet this difference was not significant.

According to these threshold durations it seems doubtful whether icons have a substantial perceptual or encoding advantage over words. The argument of Lodding (1983) and others that images are processed in parallel whereas the words in a text are processed more or less serially cannot explain a perceptual advantage of icons over single words, because usually the letters of a word are processed in parallel (for a review s. Huey, 1908; chapter 4). The argument of Lodding may pertain to the parallel perception of the constituents of a complex visual scene (Biederman, 1981) as compared to the serial processing of words in text.

Two recent studies yielded considerably larger advantages of figures over words in a nonverbal reaction task than the advantage observed by Fraisse (1968). Whitaker (1982) used as stimuli arrows pointing to the right or left or the words "RIGHT" or "LEFT". The subjects responded with their index and middle finger of the right or left hand. Responses to arrows were significantly faster than to words (780 vs. 876 ms). The first author performed a simple reaction time experiment with a cross and a diamond as stimuli in one condition and the words "KREUZ" (cross) and "RAUTE" (diamond) in a second condition. The sixteen subjects served in both conditions, and responded with the index and middle finger of their right hand. The mean reactions times were 361 ms for the figures and 431 ms for words, and this 70 ms advantage of figures over words was significant ($p < .01$).

In a search task through videotext pages Muter and Mayson (1986) compared verbal menu items with verbal items and additional pictures of the items. The added pictures significantly increased the accuracy of the search (2.8 % errors with pictures added vs. 5.6 % errors for words all one) but not the speed of the search. In the literature we could not find other experimental studies which compared words and icons in visual search or menu selection tasks.

Experimental study

Two experiments were run for comparing the usability of verbal and iconic items in menu selection and recognition. Six commands were used: Graphics, Delete, Write, Send, Show, and Print. These commands were either presented as written german words or as icons (s. fig. 1).

The first experiment used a search-and-select task, which is very similar to menu selection. In each trial the subject was first given a task, e. g., to delete a file. Then the six verbal or iconic menu items appeared on the screen, which were numbered from one to six. The subject was to select the appropriate command, e. g., Delete, and to respond via the keyboard with the number of the selected command.

The second experiment used a recognition task. The six commands were mapped onto the numbers one to six, and the subject first learned this mapping. In the recognition trials one command word or icon was presented, and the subject had to respond with the number assigned to the command. In both experiments reaction time was the main dependent variable.

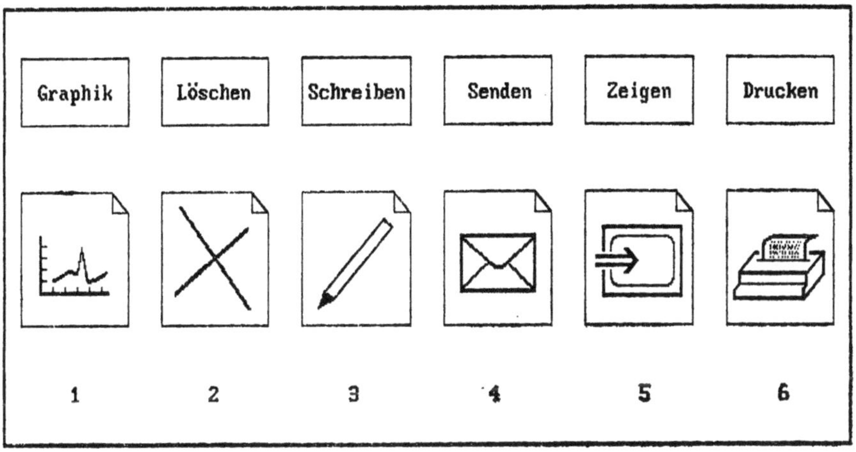

Fig. 1. Command words and icons used in both experiments

Subjects. Twelve students from the Technical University of Darmstadt served as paid subjects in both experiments. Five subjects were computer naives, and seven subjects reported having at least some experience with computers.

Apparatus and Stimuli. Both experiments were performed with an Olivetti personal computer M24 (identical to the AT&T PC 6300) with a German keyboard (Keyboard 2) and a white monochrome monitor from the same manufacturer.[1] The screen was run in graphics mode with a resolution of 640x400 pixels, and with black background color. The distance between the subject's eyes and the screen was about 60 cm, and the center of the screen was at the height of the subject's eyes. The width of the rectangular frames surrounding the command words and icons was 27 mm. The height of a word frame was 34 mm, and the height of an icon frame was 17 mm.

Design and procedure of experiment I. The experiment was run in two daily sessions lasting about one hour. Each sessions consisted of two blocks. In one block the menu items were represented iconically, and in the other block they were presented as words. For each subject the block order alternated from the first to the second session, and the block order within the first session was balanced between subjects. One to three days passed between the two sessions of a subject.

For each command two task sentences were developed (s. tab. I). The command word occurred in one task sentence but not in the other one. We expected that the command word occurring in a task sentence should facilitate the selection of the corresponding verbal menu item, which is that command word.

A trial started with a task sentence appearing on the empty screen. After 2 s the task sentence disappeared, and .5 s later the menu of six iconic or verbal items was displayed (s. fig. 1). The subject had to answer with the number below the appropriate command item by pressing the corresponding number key in the right number field of the keyboard. After the subject's response the number

Tab. I. Task sentences used in experiment I

Graphik (Graphics):
Sie möchten eine Graphik erzeugen.
(You want to make a graph.)
Sie möchten Daten zeichnen.
(You want to draw some data.)
Löschen (Delete):
Sie möchten eine Datei löschen.
(You want to delete a file.)
Sie möchten ein Dokument zerstören.
(You want to erase a document.)
Schreiben (Write):
Sie möchten in einem Dokument schreiben.
(You want to write in a document.)
Sie möchten eine Datei editieren.
(You want to edit a file.)
Senden (Send):
Sie möchten ein Dokument senden.
(You want to send a document.)
Sie möchten Daten abschicken.
(You want to dispatch some data.)
Zeigen (Show):
Sie möchten ein Dokument auf dem Bildschirm zeigen.
(You want to show a document on the screen.)
Sie möchten Daten auf dem Bildschirm ausgeben.
(You want to display some data on the screen.)
Drucken (Print):
Sie möchten ein Dokument drucken.
(You want to print a document.)
Sie möchten Daten auf Papier ausgeben.
(You want to hardcopy some data.)

below the correct menu item was underlined. If the subject had entered an incorrect number the feedback was accompanied by a tone lasting .5 s. After 2 s the screen was cleared, and 2 s later the next trial started with a new task sentence appearing on the screen.

The left to right order of the six menu items on the screen varied randomly between trials whereas the numbers below the menu items remained in ascending order from left to right (fig. 1).

A verbal or iconic block consisted of six random sequences of 48 trials where each task sentence occurred in four trials. Thus in a verbal or iconic block each task sentence was presented in altogether 24 trials. After each 48 trials the subjects had a rest of 25 s.

Before the experiment the meaning of the six commands was explained to the subjects. The subjects were instructed to respond as fast as possible but to avoid errors.

Design and procedure of experiment II. The subjects served in the second experiment one week after their last session of the first experiment. The experiment took two sessions, and each session consisted of a verbal and an iconic block.

The order of blocks in the two sessions was alternated within and balanced between subjects as in the first experiment.

A different random mapping of the six commands to the numbers one to six was used for each subject. This mapping remained constant for the verbal and iconic block. Before the first block the subjects had a few paired associate learning trials until they could respond to each command with the correct number.

A trial started with a fixation cross appearing in the center of the screen. The fixation cross disappeared after .5 s. Half a second later, one of the command words or icons (without its number) appeared in the center of the screen. After the subject's response with a number key the correct number appeared below the word or icon frame. The feedback number disappeared after 1.5 s. The next trial started 2 s later.

A verbal or iconic block consisted of four random sequences of 48 trials where each of the six commands occurred in eight trials. Each command occurred in 32 trials of a block. In every other respect the second experiment was identical to the first one.

Results

For both experiments the first 48 trials of each block were considered practice and excluded from data analysis. The remaining results of the first and second session of an experiment were lumped together. Table II presents the results averaged over the six commands. In both experiments there was a definite speed advantage of iconic commands over command words.

Tab. II. Summary of results of experiments I and II: Mean reaction times [ms] of correct responses and error percentages

Command Representation	Search-and-Select Command Word in Task Yes	No	Both	Recognition
Word	1328	1423	1375	917
	1.6	2.4	2.0	1.8
Icon	1218	1227	1223	733
	2.4	2.8	2.6	1.1

Results of experiment I. Figure 2 shows the mean correct response times which were obtained for the six commands in experiment I. A 2x6x2 analysis of variance of the correct response times was computed with type of menu items (words or icons), command, and command word occurring or not occurring in the task sentence as independent variables. Each independent variable and the three twofold interactions had significant effects ($p < .01$). The effects of the threefold interaction were not significant [$F(5,55) < 1$].

For iconic items it made virtually no difference whether the command word was included in the task sentence or not: 1218 ms vs. 1227 ms; $F(1,11) < 1$. As was expected the command word occurring in the task sentence considerably facilitated selection of that command word: 1328 ms vs. 1423 ms; $F(1,11) = 29.8$,

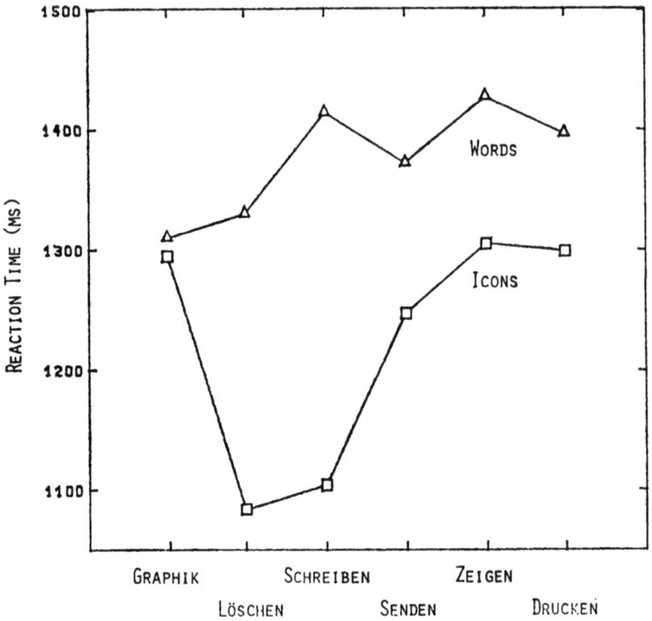

Fig. 2. Mean correct reaction times to the command words and icons in experiment I

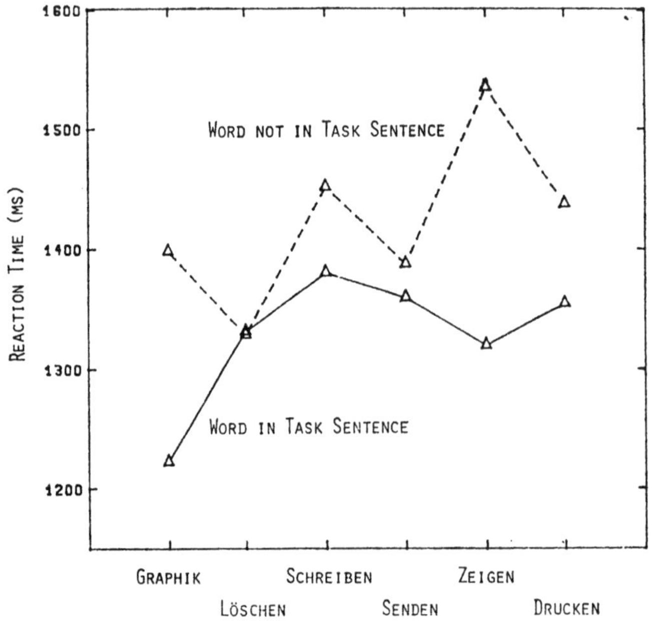

Fig. 3. Mean correct reaction times to the command words in experiment I when the command word had or had not occurred in the task sentence

$p < .005$. Figure 3 shows the pattern of reaction times for verbal menu items when the command word occurred or did not occur in the task sentence.
As a post hoc hypothesis the variance due to the different icons can mainly be attributed to the structural complexity of the icons. The two icons representing the commands Delete and Write are structurally simple, whereas the remaining four icons are structurally more complex (s. fig. 1). Structural simplicity of an icon means that it has only few distinctive global features and no local or detail features. The two structurally simple icons yielded considerably shorter reaction times than the four structurally complex icons: 1095 ms vs. 1287 ms; $F(1,55) = 79.34$, $p < .001$. Within each subset, however, the reaction time differences did not reach significance (between both structurally simple icons: $F(1,55) < 1$; between the four structurally complex items: $F(3,55) = 1.22$, $p > .3$).
A 2x6x2 analysis of variance of the error proportions yielded no significant effects except for the interaction between the commands and command word occurring or not occurring in the task sentence [$F(5,55) = 2.69$, $p < .03$].

Results of experiment II. Figure 4 shows the correct recognition times for the six commands in experiment II. A 2x6 analysis of variance of the correct response times was computed with type of item (verbal or iconic) and command as independent variables. Type of item, command and their interaction had significant effects on recognition time (type of item: $F(1,11) = 41.4$, $p < .001$; command: $F(5,55) = 3.04$, $p < .02$; type of item x command: $F(5,55) = 5.63$, $p < .001$). A 2x6 analysis of the error proportions showed no significant effects of any independent variable ($p > .19$).

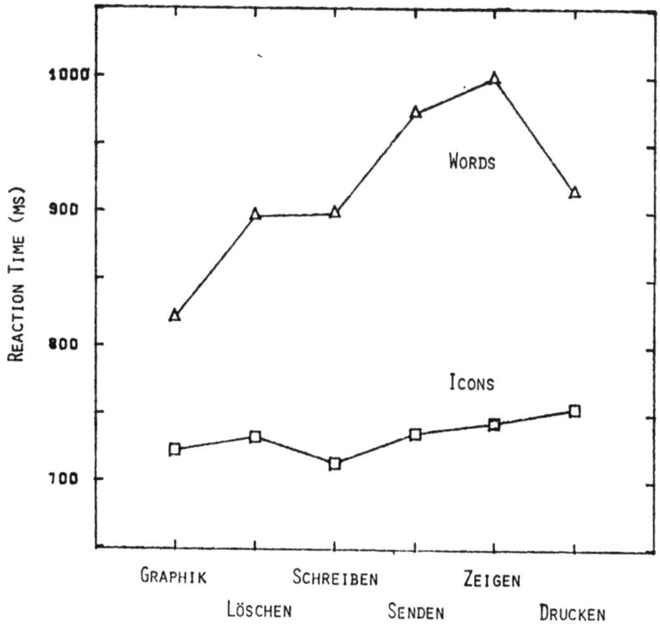

Fig. 4. Mean correct reaction times to the command words and icons in experiment II

The six iconic commands had no significant effects on response time [$F(5,55) < 1$]. In particular, the response times to the two structurally simple icons for Delete and Write were not significantly faster than to the four structurally complex icons: 723 ms vs. 739 ms; $F(1,55) = 1.15$, $p > .3$. The six command words had quite different effects on recognition time: $F(5,55) = 13.91$, $p < .01$.

Discussion

The experimental evidence for the better usability of iconic items in menu selection is quite clearcut. Even if the command word had occurred in the task sentence the selection of that command word from the menu was slower than the selection of the corresponding icon, with the exception of the Graphics command.

The observed advantage of the two structurally simple icons for Delete and Write over the four structurally more complex icons for Graphics, Send, Show, and Print suggests a possibly important principle for the construction of icons for menu selection. According to our results it is not only the communicativeness of an icon but also its structural simplicity which determines its usability in menu selection. Communicativeness of an icon is defined as how well it suggests the denoted object (Green and Pew, 1978). The two structurally simple icons for Delete and Write do not look more communicative for the denoted commands than the four structurally more complex icons. Structural simplicity of an icon can contribute to its perceptual distinctness and discriminability from other menu items and thereby facilitates the search task.

Remember that in the present study the advantage of structurally simple icons in menu selection emerged as a post hoc hypothesis to which the data conformed. Hence the effects of structural complexity of icons in menu selection have to be put under systematic investigation by independent variation of structural complexity and communicativeness.

The advantage of the iconic items over the command words, which was observed in the recognition task of experiment II conforms to the experimental evidence which was mentioned in the introduction. Contrary to the search-and-select task, in the recognition task the different icons did not have significant effects on response time. This difference between the results of both experiments seems not implausible. In the search-and-select task the perceptual distinctness or discriminability of the icons was more important than in the recognition task because here only a single icon was presented at a time whereas in the search task an icon had to be found among the altogether six items.

The observed advantage of icons over words must not be generalized to larger sets of items. In both experiments the set size was within the size of the memory span. For increasing set sizes it might become more difficult to construct icons which are reasonably simple and still discriminable from each other (for a discussion, s. Easterby, 1970).

The magnitude of the observed advantage of icons over words cannot be explained by the hypothesis that the icons were faster encoded perceptually than the words. The perceptual processing of a word takes quite less than 100 ms. Let us assume that the icons were encoded 10 or 20 ms faster than the words, which would be a very large difference if we consider the threshold durations obtained by Fraisse (1968). The observed advantage of icons over words in the recognition task was 174 ms, and this difference exceeds a conceivable difference between the encoding times for words and icons by about one order of magnitude. Hence the locus of the icon advantage has to be traced to later processing stages of response decision and response selection.

We cannot give a precise explanation of the better usability of the icons in the search-and-select and recognition task. We offer a rather speculative hypothesis which derives from the theory of signs of Ch. S. Peirce (Buchler, 1955). Recently Jervell and Olson (1985) have mentioned the relevance of the ideas of Peirce for using icons in man-machine communication.

Peirce distinguished between symbols and icons as two types of signs. A symbol like a word is a sign which refers to the denoted idea (meaning) by virtue of a rule, but the symbol does not bear any resemblance to the denoted idea. An icon "is a sign which refers to the object that it denotes merely by virtue of characters of its own" (Peirce in Buchler, 1955, p. 102). Perception of an icon implies the processing of aspects of the denoted idea. The perceptual qualities of the icon "excite analogous sensations in the mind" (Peirce in Buchler, 1955, p. 114). Therefore, according to Peirce, iconic communication is direct or immediate whereas symbolic communication is indirect and less immediate.

The hypothesis of Peirce that the icon itself conveys aspects of the denoted idea is sustained by the fact that figures can be categorized faster than words (e. g., Pellegrino, Rosinsky, Chiesi and Siegel, 1977).

Hutchins, Hollan and Norman (1986) have discussed two properties of the interface language in human-computer interaction: semantic distance and articulatory distance. Semantic distance refers to the distance between the user's intentions and the meaning of an expression. Articulatory distance refers to the distance between an expression and its meaning. The mental effort to relate a computer message (signs) to ones intentions or to transform ones intentions into an adequate expression for input increases with the semantic and articulatory distance between both.

According to Peirce the iconic command has itself aspects of the denoted command, i. e., its meaning. Hence the articulatory distance between an icon and the denoted command ought to be smaller than the articulatory distance between a command word and its meaning.

In the search-and-select task a command word or icon was selected according to the correspondence between its meaning and the subject's intentions, which was induced by the task sentence. Since the articulatory distance between an icon and its meaning is assumed to be smaller than the articulatory distance between the command word and its meaning the required mental effort for transforming the intention into the selection of an item was smaller for iconic menu items than for verbal items. This is our proposed explanation of the observed advantage of icons over words in the search-and-select task.

The foregoing reasoning can also be applied to the recognition task of experiment II. Logically, the meaning of the command words and icons was not necessarily relevant to the recognition task. The command words and icons had been mapped onto the numbers one to six, and the subjects could respond in accordance with this mapping without regard of the meaning of the command words or items. It is, however, quite implausible that the subjects ignored the meaning of the command words and icons. First, before the recognition task each subject had served in two sessions with the search-and-select task where the meaning of the menu items was relevant to the task. Second, the same number had been assigned to the word and icon denoting the same command. Third, the many experiments using the Stroop-paradigm indicate that the meaning of a sign cannot be ignored even if it interferes with the task. Because the meaning of a known word and particularly of an icon is automatically activated when reading or perceiving that sign, and because acting in response to the meaning of a sign is the dominant or even compulsive mode of human information processing, we conclude that in the recognition task the subjects selected their responses according to the meaning of the words or icons. Given this, the advantage of icons over words which was observed in the recognition task can also be explained by the smaller articulatory distance between an icon and its meaning.

This research was supported by Grant WA 419/3 from the Deutsche Forschungsgemeinschaft.

We want to thank the Deutsche Olivetti GmbH who provided us with an M24 computer for running the experiments.

References

Biedermann, I.: On the semantics of a glance at a scene. In: Perceptual Organisation. Eds.: Kubovy, M.; Pomerantz, J. R. Hillsdale, NJ: Lawrence Erlbaum Associates 1981.

Buchler, J. (Ed.): Philosophical writings of Peirce. New York: Dover Publications, Inc. 1955.

Card, S. K.; Moran, Th. P.; Newell, A.: The psychology of human-computer interaction. Hillsdale, NJ: Lawrence Erlbaum Associates 1983.

Cattell, J. McK.: Über die Zeit der Erkennung und Benennung von Schriftzeichen, Bildern und Farben. Philosoph. Stud. 2 (1885) 635–650.

Easterby, R. S.: The perception of symbols for machine displays. Ergonomics 13 (1970) 149–158.

Fraisse, P.: Motor and verbal reaction times to words and drawings. Psychon. Sci. 12 (1968) 235–236.

Green, P.; Pew, R. W.: Evaluating photographic symbols: An automotive application. Hum. Factors 20 (1978) 103–114.

Huey, E. B.: The psychology and pedagogy of reading. Cambridge, Mass.: The M.I.T. Press 1908. (Reprint 1968).

Hutchins, E. L.; Hollan, J. D.; Norman, D. A.: Direct manipulation interfaces. In: User centered system design: New perspectives in human-computer interaction. Eds.: Norman, D. A.; Draper, S. W. Hillsdale, NJ: Lawrence Erlbaum Associates 1986.

Jervell, H. R.; Olson, K. A.: Icons in man-machine communications. Behav. Inf. Technol. 4 (1985) 249–254.

Kolers, P. A.: Some formal characteristics of pictograms. Am. Sci. 57 (3) (1969) 348 to 363.

Lodding, K. N.: Iconic interfacing. IEEE Comput. Graph. Appl. 3 (March/April) (1983) 11–20.
Muter, P.; Mayson, C.: The role of graphics in item selection from menus. Behav. Inf. Technol. 5 (1986) 89–95.
Pellegrino, J. W.; Rosinski, R. R.; Chiesi, H. L.; Siegel, A.: Picture-word differences in decision latency: An analysis of single and dual memory models. Mem. Cognit. 5 (1977) 383–396.
Shneiderman, B.: Direct manipulation: A step beyond programming languages. IEEE Computer 16 (1983) (8) 57–69.
Whitacker, L. A.: Stimulus-response compatibility for left-right discriminations as a function of stimulus position. J. Exp. Psychol.: Hum. Percep. Perf. 8 (1982) 865–874.

Author's address:
Prof. Dr. J. Wandmacher
Technische Hochschule Darmstadt
Institut für Psychologie, Fachbereich 3
Hochschulstr. 1, D – 6100 Darmstadt

From the Department of Psychology, Free University Amsterdam, the Centre for Education and Information Technology Twente University of Technology, Enschede and the Information Services Centraal Beheer, Apeldoorn, the Netherlands

Learning an office system – a field study on the Development of mental models

By G. C. van der Veer, M. A. M. Felt, B. van Muylwijk
and R. J. van Biene

With 11 figures

Introduction

In this contribution some observations are presented about the phenomena of the development of mental models of a human-computer system. These observations are collected during an introductory course on an office management system. The students were all well acquainted with traditional office environments and the course intended to draw upon this experience.

Systems and models of a system

Norman (1983) makes a clear distinction between a *system* (the actual thing), the *conceptual model* of the system (a description of the system as for as the human-machine interface is concerned; an accurate and consistent representation, that is invented or developed by teacher and/or designer, according to Norman), and the *mental model* of the system (a user's evolving model, by which the user predicts the behaviour of the system in interaction with his own behaviour).

This mental model is the goal of metacommunication between a user and a system, of documentation, and of courses on systems. Norman states that mental models lack detail and are inherently unstable.

Development of mental models

The development of cognitive representations of computing systems or user-interfaces is a process in which structures in semantic memory are built or changed. These activities are generally considered to be strongly based on analogies: Known concepts and structures are related to the new situation. This process can be activated if the teacher, or any form of metacommunication (communication concerning the interaction and the human-computer interface), refers to existing semantic knowledge and schemes. Metaphors may be used to activate knowledge and act as analogies. These metaphors should be presented as such, not as actual representations of the new system (Simons, 1980). The choice of appropriate metaphors is crucial for the development of adequate mental models (Carroll and Thomas, 1982; Carroll, 1983; Clanton, 1983; Houston, 1983). In generating metaphors it should be kept in mind that the capacity of working memory is restricted to a limited number of chuncks (units of meaning that may be handled as one item and are only to be expanded when necessary). Methaphors that are too rich in composition distract too much attention and may obstruct the learning process. These have to be broken down into manageable elements when presented to the student.

Individual differences in the acquisition of mental models

Novice users of a system differ on a number of relevant features:

a. a priori knowledge
   Users who possess adequate mental models of systems that are relevant in the same or in analogous task domain as is the new system, have a good base for analogical reasoning (Wearn, 1983). These systems may be computer systems, but for a lot of task domains computerless systems (office systems e. g.) exist that cover the same tasks.
b. style of information processing
   Individual style of information processing not only results in preference for different modes of presentation of learning material and of metaphors, it also leads to individual differences in the organisation of semantic knowledge. In that respect the contrast between verbal and image representation may be relevant (Van der Veer, Van de Wolde and Van Muylwijk, 1978; Van Muylwijk, Van der Veer and Wearn, 1983). Other individual differences that might be relevant in the way novice users acquire a mental model, such as field dependancy, serial vs holistic structuring of information, general intelligence, etc., are not taken into account in this field study because of time limit reasons.

A field study

We are in the process of collecting and generating ideas on the relation between course structure (the kind of metaphors used, the modes of presentation), relevant student characteristics (knowledge and experience with related tasks and systems), the resulting mental models of the system. Careful experimentation would have been the method to choose, if not the length of even an introductory course on an office system and the expensiveness of the time of subjects (especially if they are confronted with a presupposed not optimal variant of the course) prevented this. We therefor chose to take advantage of the opportunity to observe a complete course on a brand new system, from the start of the preparations by the teacher (who himself did not know this system before). The aim of this course was the induction of a mental model of an integrated office system, to such a degree that the students (managers and leaders of different divisions of a large concern) could afterwards in a justified way take decisions about implementation of this system and organisation of their co-workers' tasks. It is important to know that this kind of system covered large areas of the task domain of these groups, so the implementation of this system would have substantial effects on the internal activities of the groups.

Conceptual model of the system

In order to design the course, a specification of the conceptual model had to be developed. The only documentation available was an installation manual (a heavy set of books that were only readable for expert users) and a quick reference guide (a small booklet containing lists of tools, functions, commands etc., each with a two-line or three-line description). The manual contained introductory descriptions and the same type of lists as presented in the guide.

It took the teacher and his assistant about three man-months together to develop a conceptual model. To give a complete specification of the conceptual model of the system would be too time consuming. We only briefly mention the general structure and the most important concepts. We realise that this can only lead to a fragmentary mental model in the mind of the audience, but we have no choice. We restrict ourselves here mainly, following Moran (1981), to what is called the *task* level and *semantic* level.

The system is intended to present an integrated set of interactive sub-systems ("tools") for office management tasks. The package consists of seven tools:
- spreadsheet,
- (relational) database manipulation,
- graphics,
- editor (text entry and formatting),
- record manager and information retrieval,
- emulator for communication with a mainframe,
- generator for individual system profile
  (colours, names, configuration, passwords),

of which the first four are the primary tools, related directly to the office tasks. The letter three administration and communication between the tasks.

The *input* mode allows the input of information, the *command* mode is automatically changed into the *edit* mode when an incorrect command is issued. In the same way an automatic change to the *point* mode occurs if that is feasible in case of certain commands.

There is a series of commands which may be used in all tools (e. g. COPY, DELETE, FORMAT, GOTO, HELP, INFO, INPUT, PRINT, OPEN, SAVE), but the syntax is not always uniform. Some of these commands communicate between the tools, others between a tool and different types of objects (like documents, pictures, graph ranges, data tables etc.). The commands may be typed, chosen from a menu or in some cases issued with a function key.

The use of functions is possible in spreadsheet and database tools.

Procedures are defined by example

Metacommunication consists of error and warning messages from the side of the system, and the HELP command from the side of the user. The system tells the user to "WAIT" when an action takes more than fraction of a second. Only some of the tools display feedback like information about what percentage of a time-consuming action is accomplished.

The educational metaphors

In order to induce an adequate mental model, association to existing semantic knowledge was the goal of the metaphors that were constructed. The metaphors appealed to the available schemes and knowledge of the traditional office tasks and office structure. Since the teacher was well aware of the individual differences between verbalisers and imagers, metaphors were developed that combined verbal and pictural elements. In fact, this development went on parallel with the formation of the conceptual model (this kind of course development is characterised by strong time pressure). The final metaphors will be described along with some remarks about their evolution.

A metaphor of the task space

This metaphor is designed in order to induce a mental model at the task level. The core of the metaphor is the management of an office, with delegation of the sub-tasks to different functionaries. The most important among them (the chief of the typing pool, the draughtsman, the calculator and documentalist) are referred to as individuals. Apart from this there are people from the communication services, from the safety department (with strange side-tasks like painting parts of the buildings in different colours), people from the record-office and a group of elderly men nicknamed "Decent Old Style" (DOS), who do almost anything for you, provided you ask them precisely.

Originally the intention was not to refer to the different functionaries, but to the rooms in which the sub-tasks take place. It turned out that it was much more natural to refer to persons about the semantics of a command, rather than sending and receiving messages from the typing pool or drawing-office.

In some cases the delegation of subtasks was quite different from the normal way in an office, e. g. dealing with modes. This problem couldn't be worked out in time for the development of the conceptual model, and the metaphor had to be adjusted accordingly.

Although the metaphor was mainly verbally presented, some visual elements were deliberately included, such as pictures of the most important functionaries (in fact representing actors in a well-known television series). Imagery was called on by referring to the spatial structure of the concern's main building.

A visual-spatial metaphor of semantics

The goal of this metaphor was to present an image representing the semantic structure of the system during the work. Starting with several trials of abstract overall schemes, portraying data flow or communication channels withing the package, and of figures representing parts that were analogous to other parts, the final solution consisted of one total view of the system (s. fig. 1), consisting of a small number of visual metaphors (icons), in which colours gave some redundant information about the difference between tools and different types of objects. Communication channels that may be chosen with the commands are represented with tubes, valves depict choices of destination associated with some of the commands. The command names and the names of the tools and objects are indicated in the picture.

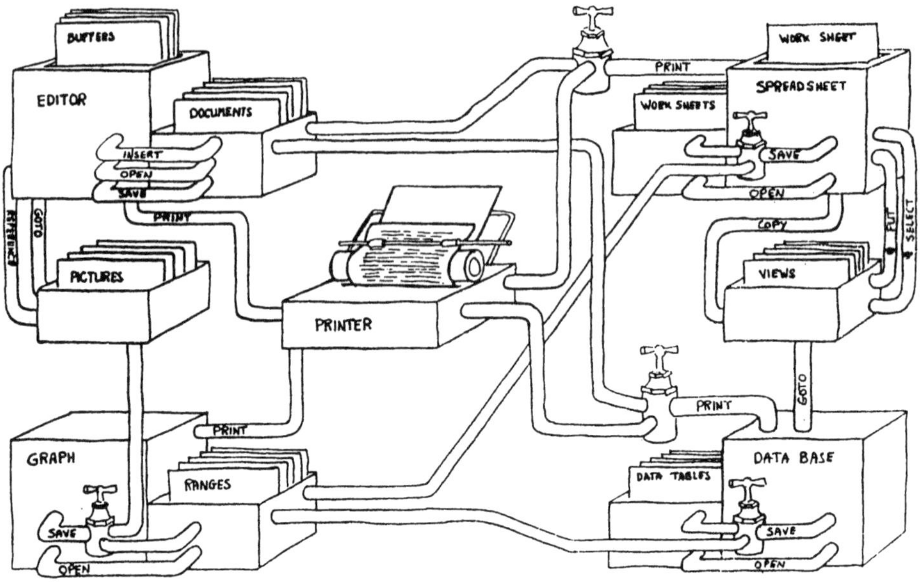

Fig. 1. Visual-spatial methaphor of the whole system

The image constructed is too complex to be comprehensible in any detail. Therefore, four sub-pictures were constructed (e. g. fig. 2), each representing a view of the system from the reference point of one tool: that is the tool actually activated at that moment. These separate views may be interpreted fully, since the number of chuncks is not too large.

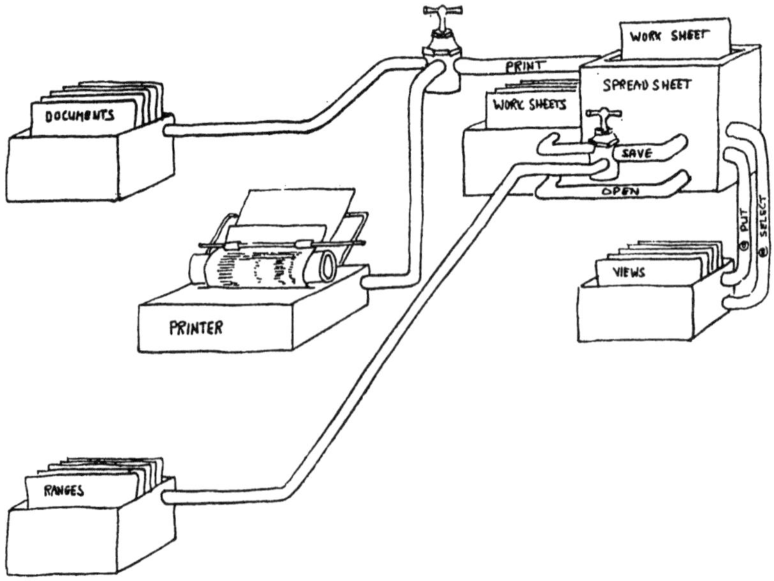

Fig. 2. Visual-spatial metaphor of a single tool

Design of the course

The course schedule is three days in a row. One half day is intended for the introduction of the metaphors and the presentation of an overview of the system, each of the main tools are devoted another half day, and the last afternoon is dedicated to an example of the use of the total system.

Introduction of the metaphors

The course starts with making the students aware of the fact that the introduction will be in the form of metaphors. The task metaphor is introduced with a general question so that the students mention the different tasks that normally are performed in an office. After the list of functions is considered complete by the teacher, the story of a very large office in a large building is told, referring to the head office of the firm in question as an analogon.

The students are asked to comment on the organisation and its efficiency, from their own point of view as managers, which gives the teacher the occasion to adjust the metaphor at places where the wrong associations turn out to be called upon. The students are told that they themselves will have to operate as a manager, and are advised to be autocratic in their behaviour, and to know exactly to which person a certain task has to be delegated.

After this discourse at task level the image representation of the semantic structure of the system is introduced. The icons are declared, and the general overview is superficially treated. It is immediately told that it is of no use to memorise all connections from this image. The fact is marked that the same commands are available at the different tools, and the function of some of them is explained for exemplificatory reasons.

The tools

Each of the tools (sub-systems) is introduced with the help of the appropriate image. Objects and commands are explained, as are the functions. For the first tool this will take more time than for the others, since most of the commands have analogous meanings, as have some of the objects. The different modes, when applicable, are covered as well.

The concepts treated are illustrated with a demonstration of their actual use with a video projector connected to the terminal of the teacher. After some of the most important concepts are covered, the students are asked to explore the tool, guided by rather global tasks. After about an hour these explorations are concluded by a group session intended to evaluate the mental model of the tool as it has developed.

The last morning of the course is partly devoted to the possibility of creating procedures, that are explained and demonstrated, but not actually practised by the students.

An integrated case study

For the last afternoon a set of data is prepared, consisting of a number of different tables about capacity and attainability of the firm's telephone exchange and network. These data have been previously downloaded from a mainframe. The instruction is to construct some relevant tables, calculate some functions, display these in an annotated figure, and insert this in a piece of text describing the relations that are reveiled. In the end the result has to be "printed", first on the screen, and afterwards on a printer.

Observations in a field study

The first possibility to collect observations was the occasion of a course in which the participating students were managers. A few days before the course took place an interview was held with each of them to get an idea of their prior knowledge, to get an impression of their intention in joining the course, and to measure some aspect of their cognitive style. During the course, observations were made of student-teacher interaction, and of the students' cooperation. At the end of the course the students were given a questionnaire to establish an indication of their mental models.

The students

There were 10 students (the maximum number that could be accomodated in the course room). The structured interview was directed at the relevant aspects of the background and at the intentions of the students.

We learned that all students either had personal experience with batch oriented systems, or did have staff members that used these. Most of them were responsible for the integration of information processing into the work of their group, and some of them designed the allocation of tasks between human resources and computers for their own office. Experience with interactive systems was less general. A few had used them to different extents. All had some knowledge of functions of personal computer applications, like text editing or spreadsheet programs, but no one had any experience with an integrated system like the one taught in the course. Some had learned one or more computer languages, but most had not used one during the last years. All students had at least some typing skill.

The students needed to know the general principles of the new system, in order to take decisions about the implementation of this or a comparable system in the work structure in their group, or in the group they advised. Most of them considered using such a system themselves, although the actual need varied. For all participants time was very scare (in fact most would have preferred to take the course during the evenings) so the investment of three days was an indication of their motivation.

In order to establish the individual style of information processing that is relevant to the mode of the metaphors presented we applied a procedure described by Van der Veer, Van de Wolde and Van Muylwijk (1978), that gave an indication of the extend to which one prefers to store an image representation, an abstract representation or a verbal episodic representation. These representations are in general evenly distributed in investigations on adult groups. In this group, 5 students turned out to have a preference for image representations, the other five displayed a mixture of the other possibilities. Since the group is so small, we decided to take this second category together and label them non-imagers.

The course

The course took place in a specially equiped room. The students were seated in pairs at a large desk with sufficient room for handling paper, and with one personal computer for each pair. The pairs were as far as possible matched on amount and type of prior knowledge, in order to prevent one of a pair from dominating the other. The teacher was not informed about the differences in prior knowledge that were measured for the individual students, but he was aware of the general level and the diversity of quality. The teacher used a large video projector to project the display of his PC, and an overhead projector for displaying material like the visual metaphor.

The introduction of the system as a whole and of the different tools always took the form of conversation and the task metaphor was elaborated first. Then the semantic image was projected, and a (black and white) copy of it was handed out. After this, and after some examples were displayed on the video screen, the students were asked to explore the possibilities that had been mentioned. At the first occasion this turned out to be somewhat difficult, as they had no clear idea how to get started, and also because there were some fundamental misconceptions that were revealed during the discussion after this exploration phase. During the exploration of the tools after the first, it was observed that the pairs started with discussing an exploration strategy, finding out which would be the interesting problems to attack and what would be a reasonable exercise.

The integrated case study at the end of the course, turned out to be very difficult in this occasion. Although all students succeeded in transporting information between the tools, to convert the objects and to manipulate the content with the help of commands and functions, half of them did not have enough time to reach the ultimate goal of combining the constructed graph in a piece of text. Only one pair had their product actually printed.

The mental models

A questionnaire was designed to get an impression of the resulting mental models. During the interview that took place before the start of the course the students were told the aim of this evaluation, and of the observations recorded during the course. They were asked to choose an identification number, and were told that the teacher would never know the identity of the individual from whom data were collected.

At the end of the course the questionnaire was handed out by the experimenter who had taken the interviews and had been present to record observations. He told the students that he wanted to know what kind of knowledge they had gathered about the system, and asked them to interpret the questions in this way. They were asked to mail the questionnaires, marked with their identification number, to the institute of the experimenter. They were not allowed to

take any official documentation about the system with them, but the experimenter promised to send them the quick reference guide as soon as he received their responses.
The topics covered by the questions can be grouped into four aspects: the use of analogies to existing knowledge, the quality at the semantic level of the resulting model, the preference for modes, and the kind of representation. For each of these aspects we give an indication of any difference we found between the "imagers" and the "nonimagers" among students. This is solely an indication of possibly interesting relations. The small number of participants does not allow to give any statistically significant assertion.

a. Analogies of semantics

The analogy between one of the possible ways of installation of tabulation and margins in an editor, and the actions on a conventional typewriter, was correctly perceived by all imagers, but only 2 of the 5 non-imagers.
The analogy of the a priori semantics of the concept "undelete" and the command UNDELETE was perceived by all but one (a non-imager) correctly. In fact this command could be used for other things apart from undoing an error, like copying and transport of fragments within an object.

b. Correctness of semantics

One of the questions asked for the difference between some related format commands. The responses contained the correct semantic distinctions in the case of all imagers, and of one non-imager. Figure 3 shows an example.

```
     This     is     verbatim.
This is fill.
This        is           justify.
```

Fig. 3. Semantic representation of some format commands

A question about the function of a list of commands and their relation to the different tools resulted in a reasonable description at the semantic level (e. g. fig. 4) for all, except one non-imager.

function		where/when/which tool
OPEN	"open" file, worksheet, etc. for input, other modifications, joining, etc. It is put into internal memory	EDITOR SPREADSHEET DATABASE GRAPH
SAVE	write a file to harddisk or floppy	idem
PRINT	information to printer for printing on paper or to the screen	SPREADSHEET GRAPHICS EDITOR
COPY	copying data from a cell or range to another location	SPREADSHEET EDITOR
INSERT	insertion of one or more rows or columns	SPREADSHEET EDITOR
GOTO	"jump" with the cursor to another location	SPREADSHEET

Fig. 4. Example of a semantic representation of relations between commands and tools

The representation of the relation between the objects and the modules or tools varied. Only some non-imagers were able to display a (very fragmentary) relation, whereas all imagers gave either an indication of any relation (fig. 5) or a semantically annotated structure (fig. 6).

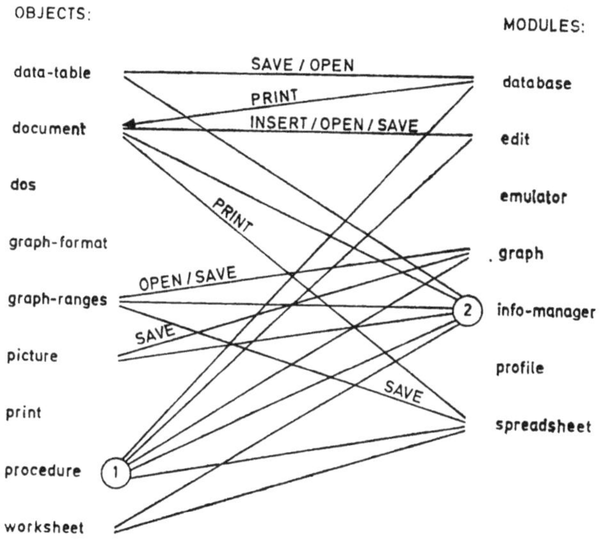

Fig. 5. **Representation of relations between objects and tools**
1 — teach mode, 2 — directory listing

A	B	
data-table	database	A = individual file in B
	spreadsheet	A = input file for B
	emulator	A via emulator to/from mainframe
	info-manager	for description
document	edit	A = individual "file" in B
	emulator	A via emulator to/from mainframe
	info-manager	for description
	spreadsheet	saved as "document" or as part of one
dos	emulator	
graph-format	graph	specifications of what is under a graph
graph-ranges	graph	columns or rows of which a graph is made
picture	graph	displays the picture
	edit	references a saved picture that e. g. is to be included in a report
print	edit	send data to screen or printer
	graph	idem
	spreadsheet	idem
procedure	database }	collects actions, stored in a "procedure" so that they can be called
	spreadsheet }	repeatedly (made with assistance of "teach")

Fig. 6. **Representation of semantic structure of objects and tools**

c. Preference for modes

In some of the tools of the system one has the possibility to choose a mode, e. g., input the coordinates of the range. All imagers preferred pointing, and only two of the non-imagers.

d. Representation of the mental model

In order to get an idea of the representation the students use of the mental model of the system, a teach-back procedure was used: The students are asked to give an overview of the transactions with the system that are needed to accomplish a certain goal, in such a way that their overview is understandable to a colleague who has either only knowledge of the traditional office procedures for this task, or, in another question, has experience with separate systems like editors or database tools.

All imagers and three non-imagers presented some kind of model for at least two of the three situations. The resulting representations are illustrative of the types of models that the students use. One represents images at task-level only (fig. 7).

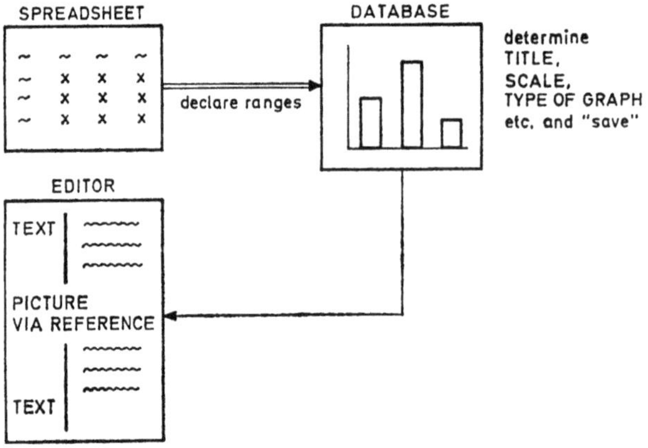

Fig. 7. Image representation at task level

One other explains the solution in terms of the verbal component of the metaphor of the task level (fig. 8),

The calculator says which parts of the worksheet are important for the draftsman.
These data are put on a separate sheet of paper (RANGES) and are sent to the draftsman.
The draftsman makes, from that paper (RANGES), a drawing and places this drawing in the typists tray.
The typist types the nota and puts the drawing in the location indicated.

Fig. 8. Verbal metaphor at task level

four of the students display a list of commands, with semantic annotations e. g. fig. 9),

1	open worksheet with SPREADSHEET
2	copy → view with SPREADSHEET
3	call "view" from GRAPH with assistance from? –statement → "range"
4	build with assistance of GRAPH/time series "PICTURE" (reference sheet)
5	build report-text with "input"
6	insert "PICTURE" (reference sheet) with EDITOR/insert

Fig. 9. Command list with semantics

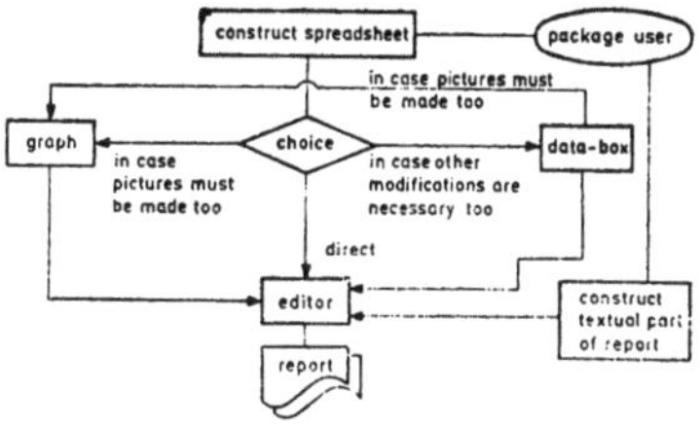

Fig. 10. Flow-chart representation with semantic.

one uses a flow-chart at the semantic level (fig. 10), and one student uses a representation at key stroke level (semantically annotated, s. fig. 11). This student explicitely states that he is unable to represent anything that would be understandable for a collegue without experience with computerised tools (which seems reasonable with his style of representation).

enter the
following: IN ↓ (go to folder of choice with arrows)
OP ↓
TO ED OP (here name of document that
↓ must be opened, and thus
must be in the buffer)
F2 WO OP (here name of spreadsheet
↓ that is to be input)
F4 indicate range with arrow ↓
TO ED indicate where spreadsheet
↓ must begin
hereafter save everything and close
or work further

Fig. 11. Key-stroke representation

Discussion and Conclusions

Research on teaching in real life situations has to cope with the restricted opportunities that teachers and students grant. Observation is often the only way to collect data that are necessary both for the development of theory, and for evaluation. In this case acquisition of realistic notions about the development of mental models was our interest. It appears possible to get an impression of the mental representation. It is striking that these representations reflect the different levels that Moran uses for his CLG. Only a syntactic representation was not found in the products of this small group.

The group of students in this field study is too small to get more than a first impression of relations between individual differences and resulting mental models. The preferred mode of representation of information as measurable on the dimension imager/non-imager seems to be relevant for the disposition of the resulting mental model. The kind of metaphors that were used in the first course, could not be varied, but we have an indication they are not too bad to induce the kind of semantic knowledge that is intended, for students that may be called imagers.

At new occasions of this course the teacher will have to apply other methods in order to take care of the problems of non-imagers. After the introduction of the metaphor at task level, an example will be handed out that shows different succesive phases in the processing of a real life task performed with the system. The different semiproducts (in fact images of objects created and handled in the system during the process) will be printed each on a separate sheet. These sheets will be stapled together in the actual order of creation by the system. No indication of the commands or the system tools will be provided on this occasion. On behalf of the non-imagers, who showed problems with the rather unstructured exploration of the different tools, alternative excercises will be provided, consisting of detailed problems that stress elaboration of syntactic structure and related semantics. These are intended to help students who prefer guided practise to free exploration of the semantic space. New observations will be collected to validate this method.

References

Carroll, J. M.: Presentation and form in user-interface architecture. Byte December 1983. P. 113–122.

Carroll, J. M.; Thomas, J. C.: Metaphor and the cognitive representation of computing systems. IEEE Trans. Syst. Man Cybernet. 12 (1982) 107–116.

Clanton, C.: The future of metaphor in man-computer systems. Byte December 1983. P. 263–270.

Houston, T.: The allegory of software. Byte December 1983. P. 210–214.

Moran, T. P.: The command language grammar: a representation for the user interface of interactive computer systems. Int. J. Man-Machine Stud. 15 (1981) 3–50.

Muylwijk, B. van; Veer, van der; Waern, Y.: On the implications of user variability in open systems. Behav. Info. Techn. 2 (1983) 313–326.

Norman, D. A.: Some observations on mental models. In: Mental Models. Eds.: Stevens, A. L.; Gentner, D. Hillsdale, N. J.: Erlbaum 1983.

Simons, P. R. J.: Vergelijkenderwijs: onderzoek naar de invloed van metaforen op het leren. Van Spaendonck drukkerij. Tilburg 1980.

Veer, G. C. van der; Muylwijk, B. van; Wolde, G. J. E. van de: Cognitive styles and differential learning capacities in paired-associate learning. In: Cognitive psychology and instruction. Eds.: Lesgold, A. M.; Pellegrino, J. W.; Fokkema, S. D.; Glaser, R. New York: Plenum Press 1978.

Waern, Y.: Prior knowledge as obstacle and help in computer aided tasks. Working papers from the cognitive seminar, 17. Department of psychology. University of Stockholm 1983.

Author's address: Dr. G. van der Veer
Vrije Universiteit, Department of Psychology
Postbox 7161, NL – 1007 MC Amsterdam

From the Department of Psychology, University of Stockholm, Sweden

On the role of models in the instruction of novice users of a word processing system[1]

By Yvonne Waern and L. Rabenius

Introduction

A problem-solving analysis of learning in a new computer environment

When novices are introduced to a computing system, the learning process will include most variants of learning studied during the history of psychology: conceptual learning, learning-by-doing and verbal learning. The complexity of the computer situation differs however from most learning situations previously studied in learning laboratories. None of the traditional learning theories are relevant alone. A new theoretical approach adapted to the complexity of the situation is required. The information processing theory offers such an approach through its analysis of problem-solving (Newell and Simon, 1972).

The editing of texts can be seen as the successive revision of an original version of a text towards an imagined goal text. The means of revision are a set of commands usually conveyed in a system manual. This way of describing the word-processing task is in line with the kind of analysis developed within the field of problem-solving. Let us take advantage of that analysis. A task to be solved is in general constituted by

1. an actual configuration of objects,
2. an anticipated goal configuration, and
3. operations for the change of configurations.

The totality of configurations that can be reached with the operations is said to form the problem space. The solution of a task can be described with a route through that problem space. In a text editing task the objects would be letters, words paragraphs etc., the configurations would be the different versions of the text; examples of operations would be insertions, deletions.

From the point of view of the problem solvers, they will have to consider:
– which the relevant objects are,
– how to implement the revisions in terms of system operations.

When novice users learn to use a particular system, they acquire knowledge related to these questions and as a consequence the problem-space gets more and

[1] This investigation has been supported by a grant from the Swedish Board of Research in the Humanities and Social Sciences. Data collection has been performed by Lars Rabenius and Christer Lindblom.

more distinct. In further learning stages, knowledge related to the choice of operations is acquired. When several operations are applicable to a particular configuration, users have to learn which one to select. Expert users have acquired such "selection rules". (cf. Card, Moran and Newell, 1980, 1983).

In a new situation, users have to obtain information about all these details: what to observe, which operations that are possible, what may be accomplished by the operations and under what conditions they may be used. In a "natural" situation, this information is given by manuals, formal tutoring, informal advisers, and the system itself. The question can now be asked: what kind of information can the users best capitalize on at different stages in their learning.

Analysis

Levels of information – types of models

At the present time, a very popular concept when talking about people's learning in general and learning in new computer situations in particular is the model (cf. Carroll and Thomas, 1982; Carrol and Mack, 1985; Norman, 1983; Williams Hollan and Stevens, 1983; Young, 1938). A model is some kind of user representation of a phenomenon. The concept is used here to convey the idea that a phenomenon is looked at and acted upon in a more or less coherent way.

A model of a system can be more or less accurate as a consequence of the quality of the information received about that system. General characteristics of a system can be high-lighted in a metaphor. Task-specific models require detailed information about the workings of the system. The introduction of metaphors and task-specific guide-lines to users do not exclude each other as means for learning the system. They have different functions and require different actions in the course of learning. To see how, let us consider three levels of information about a system.

1.: General level. The metaphor helps the users to integrate the details and frees them from having to learn each detail separately. (This is of course only valid if the metaphor is adequate for the task and system at hand, cf. Halasz and Moran, 1982). What demands must a metaphor meet in order to work well?

The first requirement of a metaphor is that the users themselves can find the relevant relations between it and reality (here the system). This requirement is a result of the fact that the metaphor is only vaguely related to the actual situation. For example, if a metaphor suggests that a word-processing system is "like a typewriter", the text on the screen might be likened to a text on a piece of paper. However, the users have to decide how to conceptualize the movement of the text on the screen. Is the screen like a window, behind which the text is moved up and down? Or is the text fixed and the screen like a window which moves up and down across the text? This is important in order to understand the commands of moving around in the text.

A further requirement is that the users must be able to make inferences and guesses at points where their model of the system is insufficient. A metaphoric model is by its nature always insufficient. One example where inferences and guessings are required can be given by the following situation:

Users have been given a typewriter metaphor for a word-processing system. The have learned that in order to delete a symbol, they have to move the cursor to the symbol and make a "delete" command. They have not yet learnt how to insert letters into already existing text. By analogy to the "delete" command and by using the typewriter metaphor, they will most probably infer that the insertion will take place at the position of the cursor. In a system where the cursor is placed on a letter (rather than between them), the model will no longer suffice. Where will the insertion take place? Before or after the letter on which the cursor is placed?

We have hitherto considered only the novice users' first attempts with the system. What happens when the first attempt fails? What use are metaphors then? Pointing to a metaphor is helpful for debugging purposes if the errors made emerge from misconceptions due to the use of an inadequate model. Errors emerging from wrong inferences or guesses from a correct model will not be helped by the metaphor.

To sum up, metaphoric models are good for users who want to avoid becoming overwhelmed by detailed information. At the same time they require the users themselves to find out the relevant relations between the metaphor and the system, to draw inferences, and to guess at points where the metaphor is insufficient. They are of little use for detailed debugging.

2.: Medium level. The construction of a detailed model requires information about the system in terms of a problem-space. Information about available operations help the users to organize the solution of the task. Unsystematic guesses are avoided by defining the problem space. Maybe the users will not always find the best way through the problem-space. They may not make the best possible use of the system, and they may perform tasks in unnecessarily complex ways. But they will at least be able to solve most tasks.

The problem-space model contains no information about the sequence of steps to be taken in order to perform a particular task. Most simple corrections turn out to need more foresight than naive users usually imagine. Replacing "re" by "regarding", for example, will need some problem-solving to avoid ending up with words like "aregarding", where "re" in "are" has been replaced.

With a problem-space model, error handling should be rather natural in a good system. Since the problem space defines a set of possible operations at each step, it should be possible for the users to "backtrack" to the last step where the result was still satisfactory. The user can then try some other operation from that step. Few systems however allow more than one step of backtracking by their UNDO facility. More problem-solving than necessary may then be required to arrive at the relevant step.

To sum up, a problem-space model should make it possible for users to handle those tasks for which its objects and operations are relevant. The error handling possibilities of such models will however depend upon the system's backtracking facilities rather than on the employed model.

3.: Detailed level. Still more task-specific are instructions about how to perform a particular task in a particular situation. This information can be called "goal-condition-action rules" (c.f. Waern, 1985). Such information is nowadays included in many manuals to novice users. Many such manual is similar to programmed-instruction. This is even more true of present online tutorials. The idea is to lead the novice users through a carefully chosen sequences of actions. Provided they follows the instructions, of problems will arise, and they will learn the correct things to do. This seems to be a wise teaching strategy, under two conditions. The first condition is that the instructions cover the tasks which the users will have to perform in the future, and the second is that the users have the patience to go through the whole chain of procedures for all conceivable future tasks. The user requirement for this kind of information does not lie in problem-solving. When having access only to carefully chosen sequences of operations, a user will encounter difficulties finding the relevant information when they want it. Most novice users do not want to go through a full tutorial of all possibilities before being able to get started with a system. Instead they want to be informed about the possibilities when they need them. Even less useful are explicit rules in a given situation, if users makes errors by following a certain rule. If the error was not predicted in the tutorial (and it is impossible to predict all errors) the users will have great difficulty in finding out what went wrong. Also, the goal-condition-action rules are difficult to use in nonpredicted situations. New tasks that are not covered by the rules, will almost always arise. In these cases the users will have to decompose and recombine the given rules in order to find an adequate way to handle the new task.

To sum up, goal-condition-action rules will lead to correct performance in the situations covered by the rules. It is easy to see that a model based upon task-specific rules bears an inherent conflict between plurality (covering many possible situations) and learnability (memory load). The more situations covered, the greater the memory load. Also, the rules will be difficult to use when new situations arise such as new tasks or erorrs.

The present study

Metaphors

The choice of metaphors was based on the following characteristics of a word-processing system:

- a word processing system is similar to a typewriter
- in a word processing system the text can be regarded as a string of positions. that letters and spaces can occupy. This string-like character of a word processing system can be captured by a building block metaphor. Letters and spaces can be represented by blocks, that are manipulated by insertions, replacement and removals.

Some critical differences between the word processing system used and the metaphors given are the following.

On a typewriter it is easy to delete old and insert new text, when their spatial extension is the same. Additions which extend beyond a line or a page often require extensive work. In a word processing system this is not so. Here additions to the text automatically move the text forwards, i. e. to the right of a line. Deletions of text automatically move the text backwards, i. e. to the left. These spatial changes of the text are inherent in the word-processing idea and are usually not high-lighted in the information given to the users.

Another great difference between a typewriter model and the word-processing system used in this study lies in the overwriting possibility of the system. When you write on a typewriter, it is not possible to type over existing text and still obtain a readable text. This is perfectly possible in the presently used system (as in many other systems). However, overwriting will succeed only if the new and the old texts have the same length. If the new text is longer than the text to be corrected, it will overwrite existing text that the user wants to keep. It is necessary to issue a second command in order to insert the rest of the new text. If the new text is shorter, some of the old text will still remain in the system. Again a second command is necessary in order to complete the task.

Thus we can see that the advantages of word-processing systems might cause difficulties due to expectations developed around a metaphor like the typwriter.

With a building block model, it is easy to think of spatial relations. This model supports the idea that an inserted new text moves the old text, although it does not tell in what direction. Deletions in a building block model might be expected to result in empty spaces. The building block model is also suited to cover the overwriting possibility. Here the overwriting may be represented by exchanging one block for another. The building block model is however totally insufficient to cover the effects of moving the cursor (which is somewhat similar to the moving of the typewheel in a type-writing model).

Our suggestion is that the typewriter metaphor would in general be more helpful for novice users. For tasks, where the spatial relationships are particularly crucial, the building block model would however be more helpful.

Manuals

In the analysis, we suggested that task-specific information would have different effects on the users possibility of handling different tasks. We shall here consider the difference between a model based on information related to a problem space and a model based on specific goal-condition-action rules.

- As representative for a problem-space oriented guide to the system we chose the traditional set-up of manuals, i. e. commands followed by their effects (command-oriented manual).
- As for the goal-condition-action rule guide to the system we chose a set-up of the following format:

Tab. I

IF	THEN
you have (configuration) and want to do (goal)	perform (action. 1) perform (action. 2) etc.

Such a manual could also be called procedure-oriented as it prescribes a fixed sequence of actions.

Tasks

The actions taken by users is a product of the kind of model they have built from the information given and the task to be performed. The choice of task is thus crucial for the study. We created tasks which should enable us to discriminate between models built from metaphors as well as manuals.

To distinguish between effects of different metaphors, tasks involving deletions and insertions of words having the same, shorter or greater lengths were created. We also created a second set of tasks, in which the spatial rearrangement of symbols was particularly important. In these tasks, numbers in a table were displaced. A correction could easily be performed by deleting blank spaces (see method section below). In these tasks we thought the building block metaphor would be helpful.

To distinguish between users having more specified models, we decided to create tasks which directly corresponded to the goal-condition-action rules (procedures), as well as new tasks, which required that these rules were decomposed and recombined. We supposed that the procedure-oriented manual would be better for the tasks designed with that manual in mind, whereas the problem space oriented manual would be better for tasks not covered by the procedures in that manual (new tasks).

In order further to stress the difference between the different models, tasks were presented in two different sessions. Tasks corresponding directly to the procedures prescribed in the condition-action rules manual were presented in the first session and spatial rearrangement tasks in the second. Thus users given a procedural manual would have the chance to learn the given procedures in the first session, whereas users given a problem space manual would have to find out the procedures themselves. In the second session both groups would have to find out the adequate procedure to solve the new tasks.

Tab. II

Variation		Hypothesis
	METAPHOR	
Typewriter or building block		Typewriter metaphor better than building-block model when spatial relationships are not critical
	MANUAL	
Command (= problem space) or procedural oriented		Procedural manuals better for tasks identical to given procedures. Command oriented manual better than procedural manual for "new" tasks
	TASKS	
Text changes or spatial rearrangements		Building block manual is better for spatial rearrangements
Task identical to procedures or new tasks		Effect of tasks-specifity as indicated above

Hypotheses

To sum up, we decided to make the following variations, and the following hypotheses related to them:

Method

Subjects

40 female psychology students were enrolled in the experiment as a part of course requirements. The advertisement for the experiment requested that the students had no prior experience with word-processing systems.

Material

1. Word processing system

Texts were displayed on a Elite 1521 terminal, which was linked up to a Prime 750 computer. The word processing program proper is named WORDS. It was developed at our institution by the system manager Bernard Devine. WORDS is a full-screen word-processing system.

2. Introductory texts

The word processing system was presented in two different styles. The first text made an analogy to the typewriter (condition T). For example: if you want to change a letter it is like lacquering the wrong letter and writing the correct one in one act. The other introduction to the system said that it was just like building rows of wooden blocks with letters on (condition B). For example: if you want to change a letter, it is just like switching the wrong block with the correct.

3. Word editing manuals

For practical purposes 6 simple word-processing commands were choosen from the comprehensive list of commands. These commands were listed in two different kinds of manuals. The first manual was to our knowledge traditional, i. e. the command is named and then explained [command-oriented manual (condition C)]. The second manual can be said to be procedure-oriented. i. e. a task is named, then the command or sequence of commands required for solving the task is listed (condition P). – We might add that the acronyms for the commands were not natural for a swedish speaker. And that the manuals as well as all other text material was in swedish.

4. Tasks

a. Preparatory tasks. This was an exercise in reading the text headline, finding commands in the manual and executing them. The tasks were only about curser movements and how to be transfered to the next task.

b. Main tasks. The text, that the subjcets were to edit, was a 24 line, 75 column long essay about car driving (the content however being irrelevant for doing the task). This text was repeated 35 times, each time with a different sort of error to be corrected. Each time the text heading read the task to be solved. Also, the line on which the error was located, was pointed at with an arrow at the left margin.

7 types of text errors were constructed for the experiment. Six of these error types were supposed to match the command list. Exemples of errors and commands are listed in the diagram below.

Tab. III

Error Type	Example text		should-be	Possible command/s		
E1	when	→	then	just type over		
E2	trafic	→	traffic	I	=	insert
E3	allways	→	always	nD	=	delete
E4	every	→	all	O+I	=	out+insert
E5	long row: car	→	motor-car	LD	=	line devide
E6	create a new (empty) line			L	=	line
E7	kill a line			K	=	kill

The seven error types made up a block. Five such blocks were constructed, each with the same type of errors (though in a different and random order).

c. Repetition tasks. The same type of text and tasks as for the base text.

d. Transfer tasks. The "text" was here columns of numbers. Typically some numbers had slided out of the column, and had to be pushed right by deleting empty space or by other means. That is there was no simple task-command relation like in the main tasks case. We constructed four types of errors and repeated them in four blocks. In each block the error types were randomly distributed.

Tab. IV

Error Type	Example	Possible command/s
T1	all numbers on a row displaced (>)	nD = delete space
T2	part of numbers out of their columns	nD + I
T3	wrong digit; change to other	just type over
T4	a row of numbers in wrong place	LD + nD

5. Data registration

Three types of data were taken. For a majority of the subjects every key stroke on the terminal were registered in a log. The second type of data was time spent reading the manual and the total time spent on the task. Registration of reading times was done in a half-automatic fashion on a ABC-80 microcomputer. Every time the subjects turned her head to where the manual lay, the experimenter pressed a key and kept it down until the subjects turned back to the terminal screen. Thirdly audio-recording of the subjects' thinking-aloud was taken.

Design

We used two dimensions to group the 40 subjects; each dimension with two values. The result is a 2 x 2 matrix, with 10 subjects in each cell. The subjects were randomly distributed to the four cells, and taken in random order.

Tab. V

		MANUAL procedure-oriented	command-oriented
METAPHOR	typewriter	TP	TC
	building blocks	BP	BC

Procedure

1. The subjects were informally asked if they had come across word processing before and if they knew what it was about. The experimenter then produced the introductory text, with the words: I have here a brief description of word processing and the system; please read it through and so that you might give an account of it to me. After this the subjects were also asked to give a summary of the commands in the words of the "typewriter" or "building blocks" metaphors.

2. The subjects were asked to take a seat at the terminal, and were helped through the preparatory text.

3. The first block of the main tasks was done under the instruction of think-aloud. The experimenter informed the subjects that he would only answer question that were technical in nature. If the subjects asked a question on how to solve the task, there was no response from the experimenter. This was all audio-recorded. Blocks n : rs 2 to 5 did not require the subjects to verbalise their thoughts and actions. During all 5 blocks a key-stroke log was kept and manual reading and execution times were registered. Log and times were also taken during the rest of the experiment.

4. The repetition was done one (or rarly two) day later. The text to edit was a copy of block 5 in the base text.

5. Before starting with the transfer text, the subjects were once again asked to go through the introduction procedure. Also, we asked the subjects to think aloud during the rest of the session. The thinking aloud was audio-recorded.

Results

The results here presented concern only time to perform each task. Think-aloud reports and log data will be presented separately.

The analysis rests on a two-step partitioning of data; we take into consideration 1/character of task 2/subject activity.

First step partition:

Part I comprises time records during block 1 of the learning session. Times include think-aloud comments made by the subject, which is not the case for the rest of the learning session.

Part II integrates data from the rest of the learning session, i. e. blocks 2 to 5, and the repetition block from session two (identical to block 5). We refer to the repetition block as block 6.

Part III consists of data from the transfer tasks. These records include think-aloud comments.

Second step partition:

Each part is further subdivided into two activities.

Activity 1: reading the manual; all references to the manual made by the subject as judged by the study leader (see procedure).

Activity 2: residual activities; the execution of commands as well as the correction of errors through key strokes. We presume that activities such as planning the solution of a task and diagnosing errors are included in residual times.

Altogether six major analysed (2x3) of data have been carried out.

An introductory remark will reduce the number of analyses relevant for presentation. As can be judged from the above, the residual activities are mixed in character; they comprise several kinds of engagements. One might have suspected from the start that this fact would bring out no clear effects; and this is certainly the case. No significant effects were produced. Nevertheless, the tendencies are in most cases in line with what the manual reading times show. The residual times are about three times greater than the manual-reding times for the part I case. They are about four times greater for the part II case and about eight times greater for the part III case. Let us now mainly concentrate on the manual-reading times.

Part I: First block of tasks

The time data for the first attempt to use the system are presented in table VI. These times are the average manual reading times for the seven tasks in the block. Notice the long time it took the subjects to read the manual (about one minute in each case). This long time indicates the difficulty encountered by the novice subjects even for these simple tasks. It should be noted that the think-aloud instruction may have added some time to the total time taken to perform the task. None of the differences between conditions is significant.

Part II: Learning session

The manual-reading times are presented in Table VI.

1. Only one of the main effects of the different conditions is significant, i. e. the difference between manuals ($F = 4.4$ $df = 1/36$; $p < 0.05$). The procedure-oriented manual resulted on an average in longer reading times than did the command-oriented manual. This effect may be due to the fact that for some tasks

Tab. VI. Manual reading times (in seconds) for the first and the second to sixth learning blocks

Metaphor	Block–1		Block–2		Block–3		Block–4		Block–5		Block–6	
	T	B	T	B	T	B	T	B	T	B	T	B
Manual												
Procedural	64	50	18	27	16	16	10	13	10	9	11	10
Command	61	79	17	24	12	8	9	6	6	3	8	7

(1 and 4), the procedure presented in the manual was not completely specified. Let us explain this.

Task 1 could be solved by a simple overwriting procedure (one letter in the word was to be corrected). This procedure was mentioned in the metaphoric introduction. The solution of first deleting and then inserting a letter was not given as a procedure. Only a procedure for whole words was specified.

Task 4 presented some extra difficulties if the procedure recommended in the procedure-oriented manual was followed. The manual instructed the user to delete a word with a word-delete command. It did not say, however, that this command also deleted one of the empty spaces around the word. This characteristic of the command requires the user who wants to insert a new word to insert not only the word but also an empty space, following it. The effect of the command and its consequent requirement was indicated in neither the procedure-oriented nor the command-oriented manual.

This insufficiency in the procedure-oriented manual caused some of the subjects considerable trouble. When they inserted a new word, without any empty space following it, they found that it coincided with the next word. They then tried to find a command for producing an empty space. However, such a command did not exist in the manual. To remedy the error, the subjects had to understand that an empty space was treated in the same way as a letter (mentioned in the metaphoric part of the manual).

The extra difficulties were shared by both groups (procedure-oriented and command-oriented). However, the procedure-oriented group had to decompose the procedures into single commands before they owned the tools for solving the tasks; this was of course not necessary for the command-oriented group.

The difficulties described here were neither foreseen nor intended by the experimenters. In order to see whether these difficulties were responsible for the longer time taken to read the procedure-oriented manual, we reanalysed the data, excluding tasks 1 (which was not explained in the procedure) and 4 (which was in completely specified in the procedure). However the results turned out to be very similar to those presented above. Thus, the deviating tasks could not be held responsible for the unexpected result that the procedure-oriented manual took a longer time to read than the command-oriented one.

The strategies described here require more manual reading than if the intended procedure is followed. In a later report we will analyse the logs of the keystrokes in order to check these explanations.

2. The next result from table VII which merits comment concerns the significant interaction between metaphor and blocks of tasks ($F = 3.4$ $df = 4/144$; $p < 0.01$). The building block metaphor resulted in longer reading times for the second block, but about the same reading time for later blocks. This implies that the building block metaphor was less adequate for the system to be learned than the typewriter metaphor; nota bene for the second block only.

3. Further, the differences between blocks of tasks are significant ($F = 26$ $df = 4/144$; $p < 0.001$). The subjects did indeed learn a lot; their reading times were reduced to about a third from the second to the fifth block.

The learning result further indicates that the metaphors given did not influence learning very much. The disadvantage of the building block model quickly disappeared. It may be supposed that the users' experience of the system, had a greater influence on their learning than the planted metaphor. Even though the metaphor was available during the whole learning session as part of the manual, it was rarely used during the solving of the tasks.

The small increase in reading times for the sixth block indicates that the subjects did not forget very much about the task within the restricted time period of the study (two days).

Part III: Transfer session

The manual-reading times for tasks in this session are presented in table VII. As for the first block the manual-reading times are only slightly longer than the corresponding reading times in the learning session. This interesting to note, since the transfer times include think-aloud comments. The learning in terms of manual-reading times is also evident, since the reading times for the last block is very similar to the last block in the learning session. The similarity of the manual reading times is worth attention, given the fact that the tasks are rather different. It indicates that reading times are affected more by the form of the manual than by the type of the task.

Tab. VII. Manual reading times (in seconds) for the four blocks of transfer tasks

Metaphor	Block–1		Block–2		Block–3		Block–4	
	T	B	T	B	T	B	T	B
Manual								
Procedural	33	36	18	16	12	8	6	7
Command	19	17	9	9	7	5	14	4

The interaction between manuals and blocks of tasks is significant ($F = 3.9$ $df = 3/108$; $p < 0.001$, two-tailed test). The average times show that the procedure-oriented manual was only difficult at the very beginning, but that its users soon learned to find their way through it even for the new tasks. The hypothesis that the building block metaphor should facilitate the users' understanding of how to perform these tasks in the system was not supported as far as the reading times are concerned.

A final remark concerning residual times: a comparison of the transfer and learning sessions, last block, indicates that the tasks of the transfer session are considerably harder to perform, since these times are longer. This holds for both types of metaphor and both types of manual.

Discussion

The results obtained contrast with current ideas about the importance of metaphors as well as from new trends in writing manuals. Metaphors do not seem to be as important for user's learning as has been suggested. Metaphors may influence the ease or difficulty of the very first encounter with a system. As the user gain experience with the system, the given metaphors seem to lose their effect.

Task-specific information seem more important than general metaphors. A user needs some detailed information in order to be able to handle a system. The new trend of giving complete procedures for accomplishing certain tasks does not seem to be helpful, however. Instead users seem to be able to make better use of instructions which require some degree of problem-solving.

How can these unexpected results be explained? Let us first attend to the slight effect of metaphors. We suggested that the building block metaphor would be rather insufficient for most word-processing tasks. This was found to be true in the beginning of the learning session, but only for reading the manuals, not for performing the tasks themselves. Why should there be such a difference? Nobody has hitherto suggested exactly when and how a user uses a given metaphor. The user must understand the metaphor itself, must relate the metaphor to the actual situation and must plan and debug actions. The results imply that a bad metaphor is difficult to understand per se and that it is difficult to relate to the actual actions, but that it does not necessarily affect planning, performing and debugging of actions.

It was also found that the difference between the metaphors was very soon extinguished. This finding may be due to the fact that users abandon the attempts to use the metaphors in their continued attempts to learn the system. Instead experience gained from the effects of their actions may become more important. If this explanation is correct, learning by doing is here a more popular learning strategy than the utilization of given information.

We also suggested that the building block metaphor would be helpful for the particular tasks chosen for the transfer session. This suggestion, however, was not supported by the data. The reason for this can be found in a close look at the subjects' actual actions. At the moment we have nothing but the study leaders' informal observations. These ar sufficient to suggest that most users did not use the most efficient approach to the problem. Instead of deleting a single blank space in order to move a whole row of numbers, they deleted each number and then inserted it again at the correct place. The interesting thing to note here is, that when they deleted one number, the rest of the numbers moved to the left. Some subjects noticed this effect, most did not. Among those who noticed the effect, only a few interpreted it to mean that they could use deletions to move the whole row to the left. This "insight" was certainly not derived from the given building-block metaphor but from their own experience while performing the task. We may perhaps say that these subjects created a "building-block model" although they never expressed it in that way.

To sum up, we suggest that metaphors may be helpful or harmful only at the very first phase of learning. They are helpful when the system functions as expected according to the metaphor and harmful otherwise. Later during their learning, users will make more use of their own experiences with the system. Again, users' expectations affect their ability to utilize given information. Users are seldom able to use unexpected information, not even when a metaphor provided highlights the critical information. This may be due to attentional restrictions in the complex situation. To maintain awareness of a metaphor at the same time as the keyboard, detailed command instructions, task and effects on the screen have to be attended to, certainly overtaxes most novice users' attentional capacities.

Where the more detailed information is concerned, users certainly need it in order to make the system function at all. We also find that the effect of different task-specific information is stronger than the effect of different metaphors and that it lasts longer during the learning phase. Why then does the procedural, most detailed and nowadays very popular kind of information take longer time to process? We supposed that a procedurally oriented information would be quicker to process and use in actual performance than information about possible commands and their effects, if the tasks given corresponded to the procedures presented. This assumption was not supported by the data. Both for manual supported tasks and for new tasks it turned out that the command-orientated manual was more quickly processed and for new tasks it was also quicker to use in actual performance.

There are probably several reasons for this deviation from our expectations. To start with, we found that the users did not follow the procedural manual as intended. Instead they made up their own approaches to the given tasks, approaches which required them to find out how the single elements in the procedures functioned. We may thus say that they had to make a command oriented manual out of the procedure oriented one, and that this took them additional time.

If users do not follow the procedures recommended, they will have greater difficulties in finding the relevant commands in a procedural manual. They will also be more likely to perform.

References

Card, S. K.; Moran, T. P.; Newell, A.: The Psychology of Human-Computer Interaction. Hillsdale, N. J.: Lawrence Erlbaum 1983.

Card, S. K.; Moran, T. P.; Newell, A.: Computer text-editing: An information-processing analysis of a routine cognitive skill. Cogn. Psychol. 12 (1980) 32–74.

Caroll, J. M.; Mack, R. L.: Metaphor, computing systems, and active learning. Int. J. Man-Machine Stud. 22 (1985) 39–57.

Caroll, J. M.; Thomas, J. C.: Metaphor and the cognitive representation of computing systems. IEEE Trans. Syst. Man Cybernet. 12 (1982) 107–116.
Douglas, S. A.; Moran, T. P.: Learning operator semantics by analogy. Proceedings of the National Conference on Artificial Intelligence. Washington, D. C. 1983.
Halasz, F.; Moran, T. P.: Analogy considered harmful. Human Factors in Computing Systems. Proceedings. Gaithersburg, Maryland 1982.
Kieras, D. E.; Polson, P. G.: An outline of a theory of the user complexity of devices and systems. Project on User complexity of devices and systems. Working Paper No. 1, 1982.
Kieras, D. E.; Polson, P. G.: An approach to the formal analysis of user complexity. Project on the user complexity of devices and systems. Working Paper No. 2. University of Arizona and University of Colorado 1982.
Newell, A.; Simon, H. A.: Human problem solving. Prentice-Hall, N. J.: Englewood Cliffs.
Norman, D. A.: Some observations on mental models. In: Mental models. Eds.: Gentner, D.; Stevens, A. L. Hillsdale, N. J.: Lawrence Erlbaum Ass. 1983.
Waern, Y.: Learning computerized tasks as related to prior task knowledge. Int. J. Man-Machine Stud. 22 (1985) 441–455.
Waern, Y.: On the implications of users' prior knowledge for human-computer interaction. In: Readings on Cognitive Ergonomics – Mind and Computers. Proceedings of the 2nd European Conference. Eds.: v. d. Veer, G. C.; Tauber, M. J.; Green, T. R. C.; Gorny, P. Berlin–Heidelberg–New York–Tokyo: Springer-Verlag 1984. P. 144–161.
Williams, M. D; Hollan, J. D.: Stevens, A. L.: Human reasoning about a simple physical system. In: Mental Models. Eds.: Gentner, D.; Stevens, A. L. Hillsdale, N. J.: Lawrence Erlbaum Ass. 1983. P. 131–153.
Young, R. M.: Surrogates and mappings: Two kinds of conceptual models for interactive devices. In: Mental models. Eds. Gentner, D.; Stevens, A. L. Hillsdale, N. J.: Lawrence Erlbaum Ass. 1983. P. 35–52.

Author's address: Dr. Yvonne Waern
University of Stockholm, Department of Psychology
S – 10691 Stockholm

From the Department of Psychology, Humboldt University, Berlin, GDR

Preknowledge and the efficiency of self-guided user's learning

By R. Schindler

With 5 figures

Introduction

Self-guided learning – that is, learning which takes place outside of the classroom, and which is largely free from external guidance – has become a topic of research in the fields of educational and training psychology. The most important reasons for this fact are: First, there is an everincreasing need for efficient training in schools and universities, as well as in institutions for adult education. Second, the number of teachers is limited, and third, there are many unsolved theoretical and methodical problems in designing external regulated and controlled training procedures which are adaptable to the individuality of the learner (Flammer, Gutman, 1977; Jenkins, 1979; Fischer, Frey and Jeuck, 1983; Mandl and Hron, 1985).

The problem is that totally self-guided learning, in which a learner is simply left alone in an environment, is a difficult matter for many pupils and a very poor use of available resources. It is generally acknowledged that this type of learning does not lead to high levels of attainment. In order to settle this conflict we have to ask for the prerequisites for efficient self-guided learning.

With regard to more recent frameworks of the concept of learning (Brown, 1984; Jenkins, 1979; Flavell, 1979) one critical point of self-guided learning is, among others, that the learner is able to select those pieces of information from the learning environment which are relevant for meeting the goal of learning. It can be assumed that this requires some kind of preknowledge about the learning domain. This is the point our research is concentrated on. With regard to user's learning we ask: Does the efficiency of self-guided user's learning depend on preknowledge that a person already has about task accomplishment be means of a computer system? The work described in this paper is based on a particular computer text-editing system.

Method

In order to investigate the relationship between the efficiency of self-guided user's learning task accomplishment by means of the text-editing system and the preexisting knowledge of a learner about the learning domain we use the method of question – asking (Flammer, 1981). This method can be regarded as a prototype of self-guided individual learning in communication with other persons, or written materials, as well as with the computer system itself.

In our experiments the subjects had to accomplish 4 different text-editing tasks (ET) by means of the device. These tasks were selected in such a way that they cover the scope of functionality of the system. Each text-editing task consisted of several subtasks (ST) each of which required different activities of the user. The sub-tasks of the text-editing tasks were partly completely different or identical or similar to each other. The order of the 4 learning tasks was given by the leader experimenter; it was the same for all subjects.

The subjects were instructed to accomplish the 4 text-editing tasks without making errors. For meeting this goal they could ask the leader of experiment for all pieces of information that they supposed as relevant for understanding task accomplishment by means of the system. In order to stress point of instruction the subjects were also asked to explain an unskilled person how the system is to operate after they had finished the self-guided learning procedure. The dialog between subjects and experimenter were recorded on tape.

Steps of investigation and results

Our first step of investigation was aimed at deriving all of the pieces of information which users of the text editor utilize – that is, which they ask for to form a knowledge structur about the system for successfully task accomplishment. In other words, we were interested in the components of the human-computer interface. Referring to Moran (1981) and Tauber (1985) the user interface of a system consists of those aspects of the system that the user comes in contact with – physically, perceptually, or conceptually. Any aspect of the system that enters the user's model is part of the human-computer interface. In order to answer the question if this components only depend on the interface realized design with regard to the text-editing tasks, or if they also depend on the pre-existing knowledge of the user we used two different groups of subjects in our first experiments. In the first group there were 6 students of psychology having no specific knowledge about neither hard- and software of interactive computer systems in general nor about text-editing systems in particular. The second group of subjects consisted of 6 students of informatics having knowledge abuot hard- and software of dialog systems, and about operating particular interactive systems but having no specific knowledge of how operate this text editor.

To meet the learning goals the subjects of both groups utilize – that is, asked for, or produce, or reproduce – 5 classes of components (s. fig. 1).

For task accomplishment these 5 classes of components are combined by the subjects to what we will call "interaction units". Interaction units are single dialog steps represented in memory of the user to accomplish a sub-task of the editing tasks. Their number and complexity change during learning.

It can be drawn from Fig. 1 that subjects of both groups above all utilize 4 types of interaction units (HE; HE, W; HE, W, (X*vX*); and HE, (X*vX*).

The first type (HE) represents that subjects only utilize the sequence of keystrokings to the keyboard.

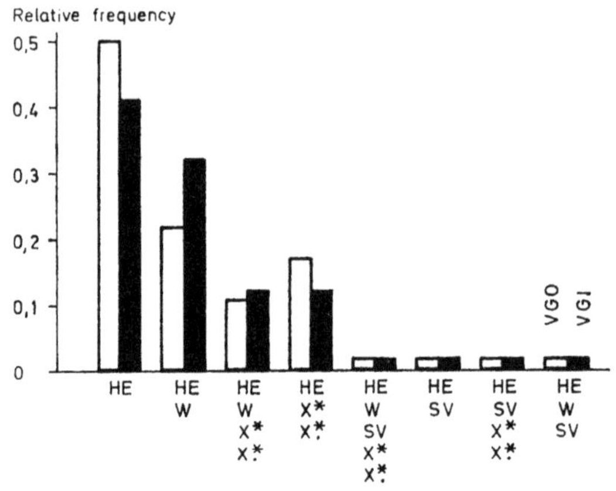

Fig. 1. Types of interaction units
HE – action units, i. e. keystroke sequences on the keyboard;
W – Word makers assigning the actual goal of the user;
X* – Combinations of alpha-numeric features displayed on screen after realizing a HE;
X* – Word markers for X.;
SV – computer processes

For instance

IF (ET: Delete word V in text Y at page N at position C
AND X: Page N of text Y is displayed on screen, cursor is at position C)

THEN (HE: press keys LÖ, WORT)

The second type (HE, W) represents that the subjects also ask for, or produce, or reproduce an actual goal of task accomplishment.

For instance

IF (ET: Delete word V in text Y at page N at position C
AND X: Monitorzeile is displayed on screen)

THEN (W: Enter commando "cal"
AND HE: Press c, a, l, FERT)

In the third type (HE, W), (X*vX*) the subjects also utilize the combination of alpha-numeric features displayed on srceen (X*) after realizing HE, or a word marker for it (X*), or both.

For instance

IF (ET: Delete word V in text X at page N at position C
AND X: Monitorzeile is displayed on screen)

THEN (W: Enter commando "cal"
AND HE: Press c, a, l, FERT
AND X*: cal is displayed on screen in capital letters)

In the fourth type (HE, ($X^* v X^*_{\cdot}$) the subjects utilize HE and X^* or $X^*_{\cdot}$ (or both) for task accomplishment. Two different cases are to be distinguished:

a) X^* or $X^*_{\cdot}$ can be only utilized to represent the result of a realized action unit – that is, they can only represent the state of the system displayed on screen – or

b) X^* or $\dot{X}^*_{\cdot}$ can represent the actual goal of the user.

For instance

Case a)

IF (ET: Delete word V in text Y at page N at position C
AND X: Page N of text Y is displayed on screen, cursor is at position C)

THEN (HE: Press LÖ, WORT, FERT
AND X^*: Word V is deleted, text is newly structured)

Case b)

IF (ET: Delete word V in text Y at page N at position C
AND X: Page N of text Y is displayed on screen, cursor at position C)

THEN (X^* = W: Word V is to deleted, text is to structured newly
AND HE: Press LÖ, Wort, FERT)

In both groups system processes (SV) which can be used by subjects to explain why a specific unit of action, or an actual individual goal (W) are to be realized for task accomplishment were utilized only very seldom. Hence, they can not be regarded as relevant components of the computer-user interface.

Two conclusions can be drawn from these results:

1. The components of the interface do not depend on the preexisting knowledge of the user.
2. System processes should not play as significant role in user's training.

In the second step of investigations we analysed the efficiency of self-guided learning of subjects having different preknowledge about task accomplishment by means of the text editor. The groups VGO and VGI served as control groups. Additional, three groups of subjects were used. Every group consisted of 6 students having no relevant preknowledge. Before starting the self-guided learning procedure by question-asking the subjects of one group – group VGR – had to learn 8 generalized rules for task accomplishment.

These rules were constructed by generalization over the components of the whole number of dialog steps which are to be realized by the subjects to accomplish the 4 editing-tasks. They can be regarded as schematic interaction units which consists of classified components of the user interface. System processes were not taken into account.

For instance

Rule 1

IF (X: On screen is displayed a word and behind it there are 6 (or smaller than 6) marked positions and cursor is located at the first of the marked position

AND W: Your goal is to input a string to fill up all positions)

THEN (HE: You have to press particular numeric keys and afterwards the key FERT)

The actual state of the system were instructed not only verbally (X) but also by presenting schematic screen layouts (X.). To test the understanding of this 8 rules the subjects were given concrete screen layouts and sub-editing tasks and they had to write down the order of classes of keys which had to be pressed down by them to accomplish the sub-tasks correctly.

The other two groups learnt task-oriented knowledge, that is, they were instructed by the experimenter how the first editing task (ET 1) is to be accomplished correctly. One of these task-oriented group (VGT_1) learnt task accomplishment by instructing the goal (W), the system process (SV), the action unit (HE), and the alpha-numeric features (X*) displayed on screen after realizing the action unit of every sub-task that the editing-task consists of. The second task-oriented group (VGT_2) were only instructed the action unit (HE), system processes (SV), and the resulting alpha-numeric features (X*) displayed on screen.

Afterwards, the experimental procedure was the same for all 5 groups of subjects: All groups had to learn the accomplishment of the other 3 editing tasks by question asking untill they met a particular learning criterion. So, the number of repetitions of the same editing task depended on progress of individual learning.

After finishing this learning procedure each group had to solve a post test which consisted of particular sub-tasks of the editing tasks learnt.

To assess efficiency of learning the number of sub-tasks to meet the learning criterion were counted (s. fig. 2).

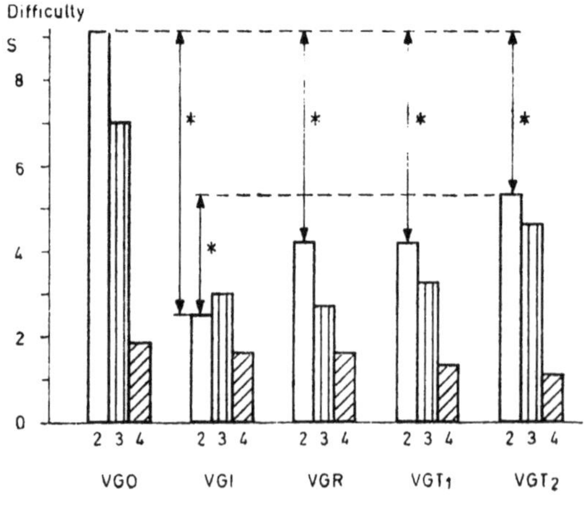

Fig. 2. Efficiency of self-guided learning and preknowledge

There are no significant differences in learning efficiency between the groups VGI, VGR, and VGT_1 but only between VGO and VGI, and VGT_2 and VGI. This is only true with respect to ET_2.

An other appropriate criterion to assess the influence of preknowledge on self-guided learning is the difficulty of learning tasks (s. fig. 3).

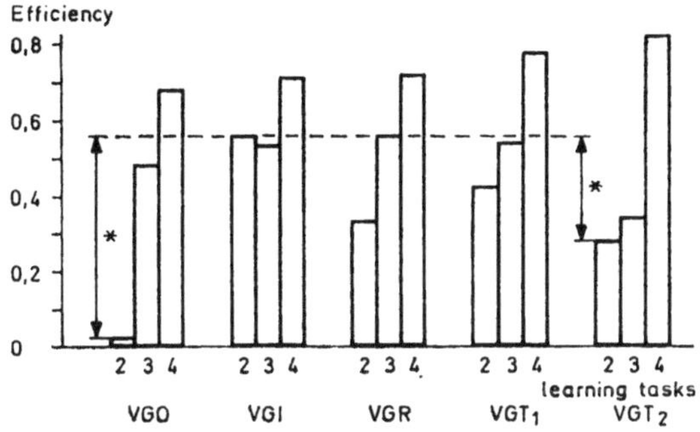

Fig. 3. Difficulty of self-guided learning and preknowledge
Difficulty (S) were counted by
$S = \sum_i i \times h\ (ST\text{-})$;
i = number of repitition a learning task to meet the learning criterion;
h (ST-) = number of unsolved sub-tasks

It can be seen in Fig. 3 that the second learning task (ET_2) is more difficult for the subjects of the group without any relevant preknowledge (VGO) than for the other groups. Furthermore, this task is also more difficult for the group VGT_2 than for VGI.

After finishing the learning procedure all groups had to solve a post test. The results are shown in figure 4.

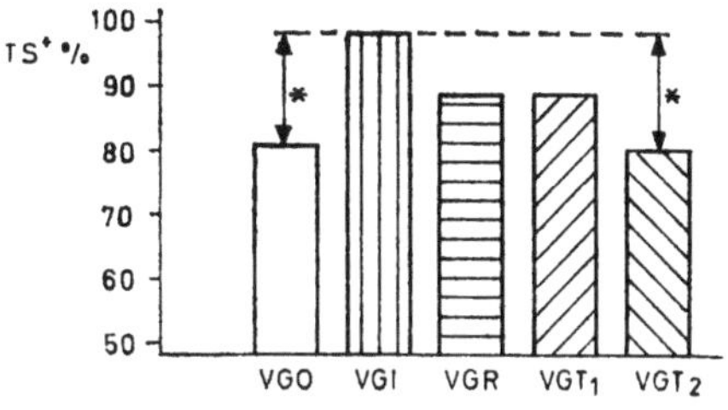

Fig. 4. Performance in accomplishing the post test

It can be seen in figure 4 that the performance of the groups VGO and VGT_2 in accomplishing the post test is significantly lower than the performance of the students of informatics (VGI).

From the results obtained in the second step of investigations we can draw the following conclusions:

1. The efficiency and difficulty of self-guided learning depend on the preknowledge that the learner already has about the learning domain. That means, self-guided user's learning can be make more effective if the user at first has to acquire a particular knowledge about the domain.
2. It makes no difference if this preknowledge is task-oriented or if it consists of generalized rules for task accomplishment.
3. We can repeat the conclusion which we had drawn from the results of the first step of investigation: system processes are of little importance for user's learning.

At the end of my paper let me very briefly discuss the following point: It could be shown by experimental results that – very roughly speaking – the students of informatics were in advance in meeting the learning goals compared to the other groups. Although, user's training will never realize by instruction techniques the knowledge that this students have acquired it is worth to ask – to make users learning as efficient as possible – for the reasons of this advantage. Our research is also aimed at answering this question but up to now we have no finished analysis of all experimental results obtained. Therefore, I can only explain one result that seems to be very interesting.

At the very beginning of my paper I have mentioned that the selection of those pieces of information from the environment which are relevant for task accomplishment can be regarded as one critical point of self-guided learning. So, the question arises if the advantage of the students of informatics is, among others, based on a better selection of relevant information.

The number of different types of interaction units utilized by the subjects to accomplish the task can be used as a rough criterion to check this question. At present we have analyzed the groups VGO and VGR and compared their data with that of the students of informatics. Here are the results (s. fig. 5).

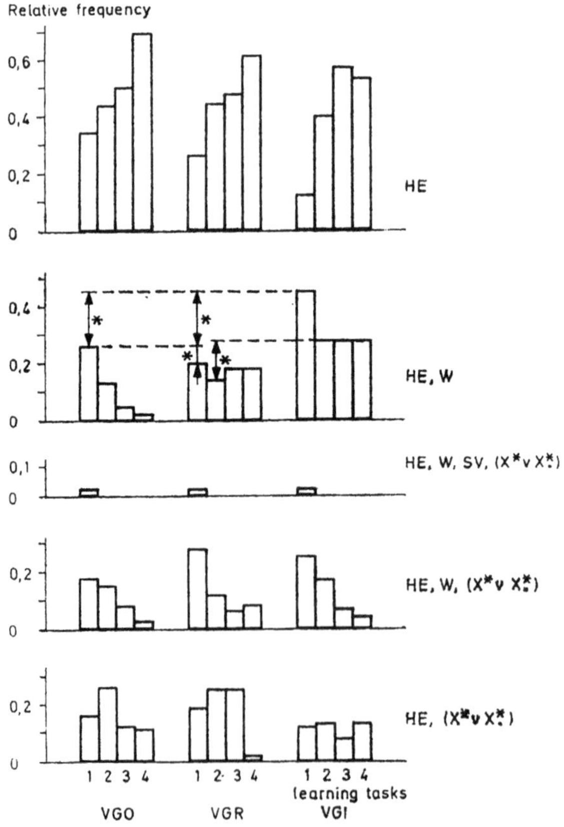

Fig. 5. Relative frequencies of interaction units and preknowledge

To accomplish the first two learning tasks the students of informatics utilized to a greater extent than the other two groups a combination of HE and W. So, the hypothesis arises if this type of interaction unit is the most approriate one to tackle the learning tasks, that means, to form an efficient internal structure for task accomplishment by means of the device. This hypothesis will be tested in our next experimental investigations.

References

Brown, A. L.: Metakognition, Handlungskontrolle, Selbststeuerung und andere noch geheimnisvollere Mechanismen. In: Metakognition, Motivation und Lernen. Eds.: Weinert, F. E.; Kluwe, R. H. Stuttgart–Berlin–Mainz–Köln: Springer-Verlag 1984.
Fischer, P. M.; Frey, H. D.; Jeuck, J.: Entwicklung und Erprobung eines computerunterstützten Video-Instruktionssystems für den naturwissenschaftlichen Unterricht. Forschungsbericht Nr. 22. Tübingen: Deutsches Institut für Fernstudien 1983.
Flammer, A.; Gutmann, W.: Das Prinzip der Subsidarität in der pädagogischen Diagnostik. In: Diagnose von Lernprozessen Ed.: Garten, H. W. Braunschweig: Westermann 1977. S. 88–96.
Flammer, A.: Towards a Theorie of Question Asking. Psychol. Res. 43 (1981) 407–420.
Flavell, J. H.: Kognitive Entwicklung. Stuttgart: Klett-Cotta 1979.
Jenkins, J. J.: Four points to remember: A tetrahedal model and memory experiments. In: Levels of Processing in human memory. Eds.: Cerman, L. S.; Crack, F. I. N. Hillsdale, N. J.: Erlbaum 1979. S. 429–446.
Mandl, H.; Hron, A.: Förderung kognitiver Fähigkeiten und des Wissenerwerbs durch computerunterstütztes Lernen. Forschungsbericht Nr. 33. Tübingen: Deutsches Institut für Fernstudien 1985.
Moran, T. P.: The command Language Grammar: a representation for the user interface of interactive computer systems. Int. J. Man-Machine Stud. 15 (1981) 9–50
Tauber, M.: An Approach to Metakognition in Human-Computer-Interaction. In: Macinter I. Eds.: Klix, F.; Wandke, H. Amsterdam–New York–Oxford–Tokyo: North-Holland 1986. S. 35–49.

Author's address: Dr. R. Schindler
Bereich Arbeits- und Ingenieurpsychologie
Sektion Psychologie der Humboldt-Universität
Oranienburger Str. 19, Berlin DDR – 1020

From the Department of Psychology, Humboldt University Berlin, GDR

Approaches for analysing and designing computer aided problem solving processes

By Elke Wetzenstein-Ollenschläger, B. Krause and H. Hagendorf

With 6 figures

Formulation of some problems

Computer assisted problem solving is a special type of man-computer interaction. Solving a problem is characterized by using the computer as a tool for reaching the goal intented by the user. According to this point of view the computer is carrying out functions like search of information in data bases, computing or creating design documentations. The output of the computer is used in reaching the goal of the problem solving process. So we look at the computer as a device for supporting the process of searching a solution for a problem. In order to fulfill this function the computer has to contain a knowledge base which has relevance for solving the class of problems considered. Beside the knowledge base software tools must be available for deriving information from this knowledge base. This is the general framework within which we analyse computer assisted problem solving processes from the point of view of psychology.

At present a lot of effort is devoted to the development of CAD-systems a special type of man-computer-systems, too. According to Jansen et al. (1985) most of the CAD-systems are mainly concerned with the generation of the design documentation and not with supporting the design process itself. In the context of this paper the design process is the most interesting aspect in which designer and computer assist each other. Phases of this process are characterized as man-computer-interaction. Therefore knowledge on man-computer problem solving in general as well as knowledge on the design process is necessary (Jansen et al., 1985; Müller, 1985) which requires interdisciplinary research.

One starting point of our approach is the characterization of a CAD-system by Seidel, 1985). A CAD-system is decomposed in three main components:

- CAD-software which is independent from the problems worked on with the systems.
- Software for working on classes of models, which is independent of objects.
- Data structures and programmes depending on objects and on the design process.

According to Seidel (1985) some of the main questions consist in characterizing contents and forms of models, which are useful, as well as in creating a software for working on classes of models. On the basis of answering those questions it should be possible to organize an efficient multiple-step problem solving process for design.

These establishements by designers and users of CAD-systems characterize exactly those aspects of CAD-systems which can be worked on by using results of psychology. Some of the potential contributions of psychology for designing computer-assisted problem solving processes are the following:

a) If we look at the system one of the main questions is the organization of the data base as well as the access to information in this data base. Quality of access, time parameters of the access process as well as output of information are determined by the design of the system.

b) If we look at the user the main questions are training for using such systems and the design of the interface. Those aspects determine the efficiency of man-computer interaction as well as the time for gaining knowledge necessary for using the system as a tool in the problem solving process (Streitz, 1986).

Methodological Approach

According to the discussion in point 1 an important aspect is the improvement of the man-computer interface by creating appropriate software tools. The task of the user is than to specify an action sequence for using these tools. This specification of desired actions has often to be described as an expression in an interface language. Our approach is aimed at developing theoretical models to understand what the user is doing when he is trying to transform a preplanned action sequence for achieving a certain goal in an expression of an interface language. The preplanned action sequence is a characterization of the solution process in the problem domain considered. The general hypothesis is that the semantic distance between the preplanned action sequence and the corresponding expression in the interface language determines features of the process of achieving the intented goal (Streitz, 1986; Norman, 1986). The solution process should be more efficient if the process of mapping units of the preplanned action process as a result of problem solving into the command set of the interface language is easy. To put it into other words, the efficiency of the computer-assisted problem solving process is dependent on the cognitive compatibility, that means of compatibility in the lexicons used for expressing results of cognitive processes.

As Waern (1986) has demonstrated we have to take into consideration the prior knowledge on solving the problems without computers. In dependence on the level of experience the process of solving a problem with a computer can be understood as a process of transforming a solution strategy known from problem solving experience without computers into an interface language or as a real interactive problem solving process where specifying the strategy is dependent on gaining information from the computer. Along this dimension users change their own conceptualizations of problems. How can we approach these problems from the point of view of psychology? One of the main starting points is the characterization of computer assisted problem solving as a kind of synthesis of problem solving without computers and the goal-dependent use of software tools available on the computer. The main question which has to be answered by psychology is how the problem solving process is modified and reshaped by using such software tools. In this computer-assisted problem solving process interaction between man and computer has to be analysed in dependence on abilities of users as well as classes of tasks.

Without further discussion we restrict us in the following on this aspect of problem solving. The following questions are to be answered by the psychology of problem solving:

- How can acquisition and use of knowledge in problem solving be characterized and analysed? What are the main determinants of building up efficient decision structures in dependence on the problem? Here we can apply results from memory research (Klix, 1986).
- How can formation and modification of problem representations be characterized in dependence on classes of problems as well as on the structure of the dialogue (see for the first aspect Krause et al., 1985).
- What are the causes of interindividual differences in solving problems? Interaction between individual prerequisites for skilled performance and information processing in the formation of problem representations and desicion structures has to be understood because this interaction is one determinant of the solution process.

The question is now, how this analysis can be performed in real situations and experiments. Therefore we turn to our experimental approaches. We will shortly characterize our approach used and present some first results gained with three different paradigms and corresponding methods of data analysis. With these results we will demonstrate what the way could be for solving the compatibility problem formulated above. Here are the three paradigms:

1. Our first paradigm is designing a simple device without the aid of a computer. Studies with this paradigm are aimed at the analyses of necessary knowledge compartments and the main stages of the process in reaching the solution. On the basis of such results we will characterize the knowledge basis and their interactions for classes of problems. This is a task for the future and could be the basis for knowledge-based CAD-systems.
2. In the second paradigm we consider the specification of a procedure for computing some function in an interface language. It is a kind of simple programming. Especially we are interested how different induced knowledge structures influence the process of specifying the command sequence in the interface language. This investigations are aimed at developing means for assessing compatibility mentioned above.
3. Because of the role of graphical interaction in CAD-systems we consider the problem of creating a desired geometrical object on the screen by transforming the intentions of the user in instructions for the computer. These investigations are aimed at gaining knowledge on the interaction of task parameters, interface language, prior knowledge of the user and problem solving strategies.

Experimental Investigations

Solving a simple design task without the aid of computers

Arndt (1985) carried out a first analysis of a process of solving a simple design task. Subjects had to design a rotation symmetrical part of a machine. The function of this part was to hold some work piece between centres. Subjects got a task description and a drawing containing all necessary information on the kind of the work-piece, on working-on procedures, on the measures of the work-piece and their allowed deviations (fig. 1, Part A, B and C). The task of the subjects was to specify a hand sketch of the work-holder, to specify the main components and to prepare a list of all components.

The analyses has been concentrated on the hand sketches in various phases of the design process and of the verbalizations during the process of approaching the solution. Four experienced designers took part in this investigation. The solutions offered by the subjects have been evaluated on the basis of a list of 5 criteria. This list has been developed by design experts. Together with experts we computed for each solution a quality index. Some of the results of this analysis can be summarized as follows:

1. To a great extent the quality of the solution is dependent on the recognition of the three main subfunctions of the part to be constructed as well the completeness in taking into consideration these subfunctions in constructing the part. On figure 1 (part D) the main subfunctions are named for one solution of the task. Each constraint-satisfying solution had to fulfill the following subfunctions: holding, setting up, guiding.

   Subjects with a high index of solution quality spent more of their activities on working on these three functions (87,7 %) than those with lower index of solution quality (66,7 %). Subjects reaching a solution with low index are more engaged in other activities such as selection of material, dimensioning, improving surface quality etc.

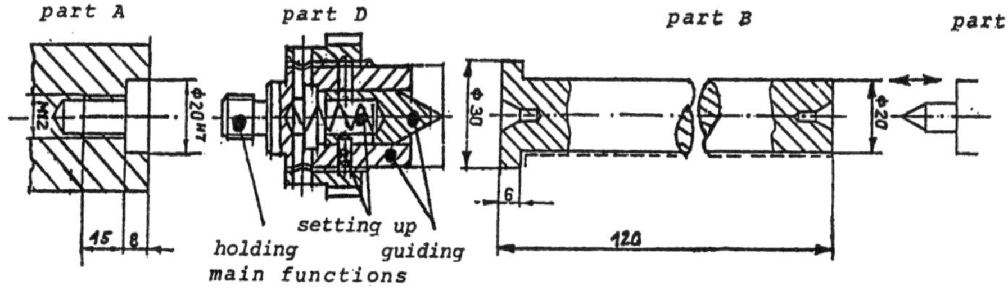

Fig. 1. Sketch of parts A, B and C, given additionally to task description for a work-holding device. Part D is the solution of the task by one subject (mainfunctions of the solution are holding, setting up, guiding)

2. The frequency of transition from one subfunction to another one as well as the moment of transitions along the time scale of the process are also very important for the quality of the solution. As we can learn from table I subjects having reached a high index of solution quality realize a lot of transi-

tions between processes of decision making (related to the main subfunctions) and carry out transitions between goal formation and decision making to a lesser extent. The most important processes are those of information search and of structuring of information for specifying the corresponding subfunction as well as for determining the moment for the transition to some other subfunction.

Tab. I. Relationship between index of solution quality and some characteristics of the solution process

Solution index (points)	Rank of subject	Time for solution (min)	Steps (number)	Subgoals (number)	Transitions DS/DS	GF/DS/GF
34,6	1.	43	29	6	10	4
28,4	2.	16	28	6	10	12
25,2	3.	24	39	10	7	15
19,05	4.	27	24	5	5	16

(DS = decision structure, GF = goal formation)

3. Formal characteristics of the solution process such as time of solution, number of activities for information search and structuring of information as well as number of subgoals are in no monotonious relationship with the solution index. As table 1 shows there seems to be a task dependent optimal value for the number of solution steps and for the number of subgoals. These results demonstrate that a deeper understanding of the problem solving behaviour cannot be reached by a formal analysis of the solution process. What is necessary is a thorough diagnosis of the knowledge available by the problem solver. This knowledge is of great importance for taking into focus of attention the subfunctions and for determining the appropriate moment of shift from one subfunction to the other in the solution process.

On the basis of this analysis we have developed a hypothetical model of the task and prerequisite knowledge. In further studies we will concentrate on checking this hypothetical model. The aim is to come to assertions on what information of the knowledge base at which moment is used and how this shapes the problem solving process. So we hope to come to a better understanding of one aspect of the problem solving process of design as a basis for improving tools which the designer has at his disposal in computerized processes.

Simple programming problems

We look at programming a computer as a problem solving process. It is assumed that the solution of a problem will be specified on a mental level. This solution has to be transformed in an expression of a computer language. It means that the problem solver has to generate a text on the basis of a notational system with restrictions (Rich, 1985). In relation to our hypothesis it follows that the difficulty of generating this text on the basis of the programming language is dependent on the compatibility of elements in the solution plan and elements in the lexicon of the programming language. In a first investigation Vorwerg (1985) checked the influence of the distance characterizing this mapping on the process of generating this text. The hypothesis was that different solution procedures for a task specified at the mental level result in different program structures. The main idea was to induce those solution procedures by solving a task without computers.

To check this hypothesis Vorwerg (1985) selected as a simple task the computation of covariance. Each of two training groups of subjects had to compute the covariance for a set of data on the basis of a different formula which was given. Subjects had at their disposal only a computer with the basic functions (addition, subtraction, multiplication). Both formulas are presented on figure 2. Then

$$F(x, y) = \sum_{i=1}^{N} x_i \, y_i - \frac{1}{N} \left(\sum_{i=1}^{N} x_i \right) \cdot \left(\sum_{i=1}^{N} y_i \right)$$

$$F(x, y) = \sum_{i=1}^{N} \left(x_i - \frac{1}{N} \sum_{i=1}^{N} x_i \right) \cdot \left(y_i - \frac{1}{N} \sum_{i=1}^{N} y_i \right)$$

Fig. 2. Variants of formulas used in the programming task

both groups had to acquire a simple programming language (fig.3). This language contained beside some simple commands two complex commands. One complex command was compatible with one complex solution step in the computation according to formula 1, the other command was compatible with a step in the solution procedure according to formula 2 (fig. 3). After acquiring this language

Simple commands

M (A)	Store A
R (A)	Read A from memory
A = S (BI)	Add B_i for i = 1 to N. The result is denoted by A.
C = C + D	Recompute C by adding D.
A = A − B	Recompute A by subtracting B.
C = A x B	Compute C by A times B.
Für I < N + 1 op_1 sonst op_2	Execute the operations op_1 as long as I < N + 1. Execute op_2 else

Complex commands

A = S (AI–BI)	Add all products A_i B_i for i = 1 to N. The result is denoted by A (compatible to formula 1).
AI = AI − B	Recompute AI by subtracting B for i = 1 to N (compatible to formula 2)

Fig. 3. Commands of a simple programming language

subjects had to write a program. Each training group was divided in two subgroups C and IC. The C groups had no restrictions in selecting the formula for their computation. We were interested what formula they selected and what commands for expressing the solution procedure they used. The other groups IC had been forced to use the formula which has *not* been used in the training session. Here we expected more difficulties in specifying the command sequence because the available solution procedure from the training session was incompatible with the formula they were forced to use in the programming task. Sub-

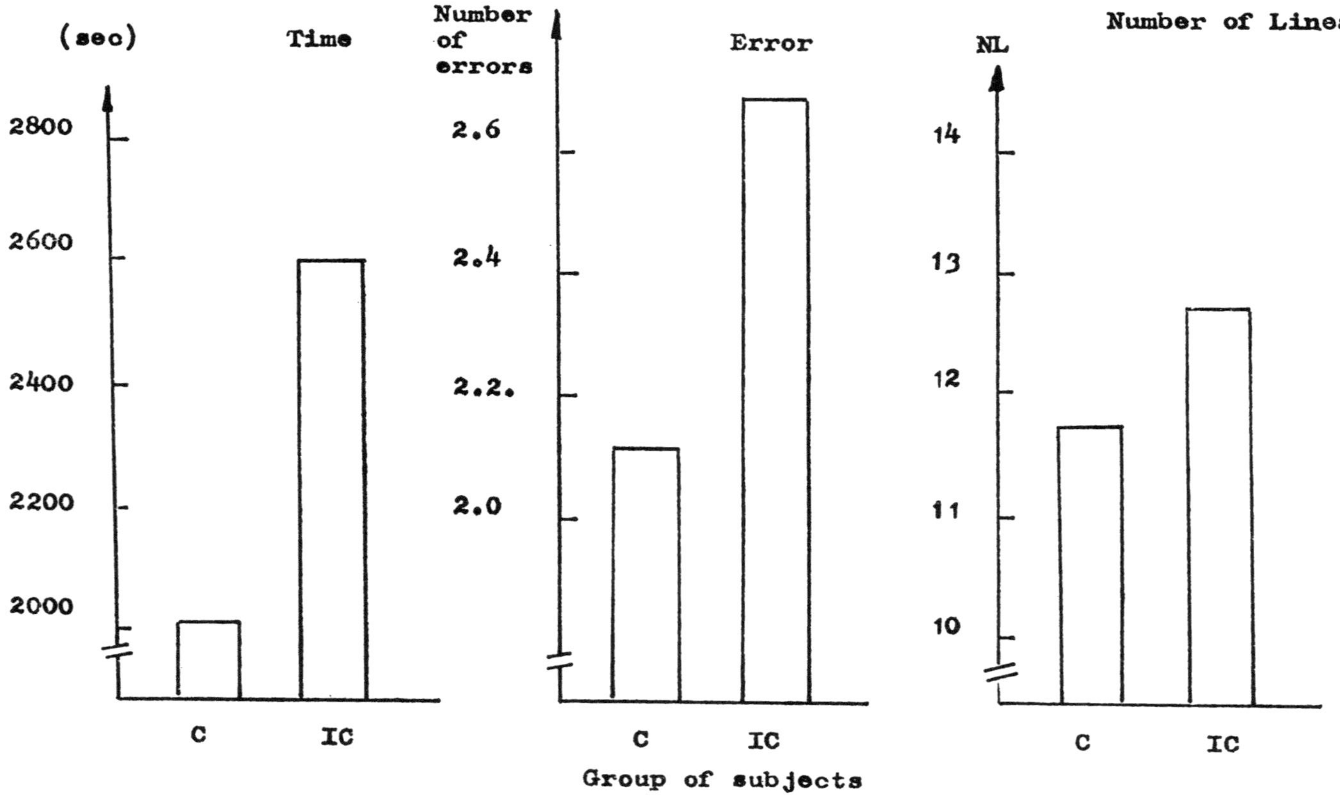

Fig. 4. Performance characteristics for group C (free choice of formula) and group IC (forced choice of formula)

jects had to specify the sequence of commands in interactive mode at a computer. Here are some of the results:

a) Subgroups C which could select the formula according their needs and pre-knowledge developed the program in about 90 % of the cases on the basis of the formula from the training session. This means the induced solution plan in the training session influenced the process of specifying the command sequence.

b) On figure 4 some parameters of problem solving performance are presented. From these data we can learn that the subjects of group C reached better performances than the subjects of group IC, as we expected according to the compatibility hypothesis.

c) We expected that subjects in group C select the compatible command to a greater extent than subjects of group IC. Unfortunately there was no unique effect because subjects in group C tend to realize the more easy structure of formula 1. Therefore Litke and Lässig (1985) carried out a similar experiment,

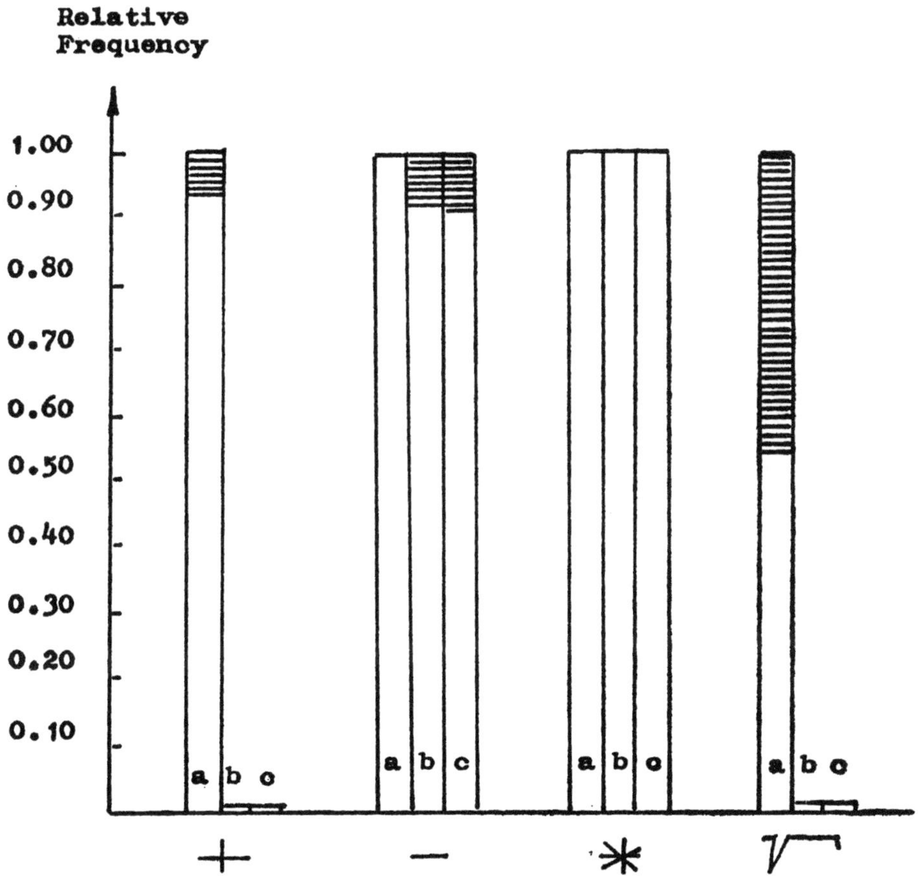

Fig. 5. Relative frequency of using compatible commands. Striped parts of columns mark differences between expected and realized behaviour

where the knowledge structure for two comparable analytic expressions had been induced by a geometeric representation of their content. Regarding the mean of using the corresponding compatible commands small differences between optimal (expected) and realized behaviour have been observed (fig. 5).

To sum up, these result demonstrate that the solution plan, induced by computing one example, determined the process of specifying the program. Subjects with were not allowed to use the plan developed in the training phase had a worser performance.

Creating a desired geometrical object

One of the characteristics of man-computer interaction in CAD-systems is the use of graphical interfaces. Gumm (1986) carried out some investigations aimed at analyzing the process of transforming the intentions of a user in instructions for the computer. The task used was creating some line drawings on computer screen. Subjects had to do this by using a subset of LOGO with three groups of commands:

Group 1: This commands allow the create a line drawing step by step by drawing lines characterized by their length and direction.

Group 2: There was only one command. With this command subjects could realize a repetition of a subset of commands of the first group. Applying this command requires a process of inducing the repetitional structure of the line drawing.

Group 3: There was also only one command, which could be used for creating new commands. So users could adapt the language to their needs and to the tasks.

Two groups of subjects acquired this language and had then to write command sequences for four figures. The hypotheses we wanted to check was that strategy choice for specifying the command sequence is dependent on the memory load characterized by planning activities and operations in mental imagery (Hagendorf et al., 1986) as well as the number of commands. To check this hypothesis we had to influence memory load. Two variables were used: (1) complexity of figures, (2) availability of the drawings during the process. In an independent experiment we got values for complexity on the basis of applying a scaling procedure and by measuring encoding time for drawings (Kyllonen et al., 1984). To vary the second variable one of the two groups had the drawings available during programming and the other group hat to program the drawing on the basis of information in the visual buffer.

In deriving the solution subjects can use at least two strategies:

1. Strategy A is a step-by-step strategy which is based only on commands of group 1. This strategy requires low planning effort but a high number of commands.
2. Strategy C is a top-down strategy where subjects specify the procedure by using also the commands of the two other groups. This results in high planning effort but in a lower number of commands.

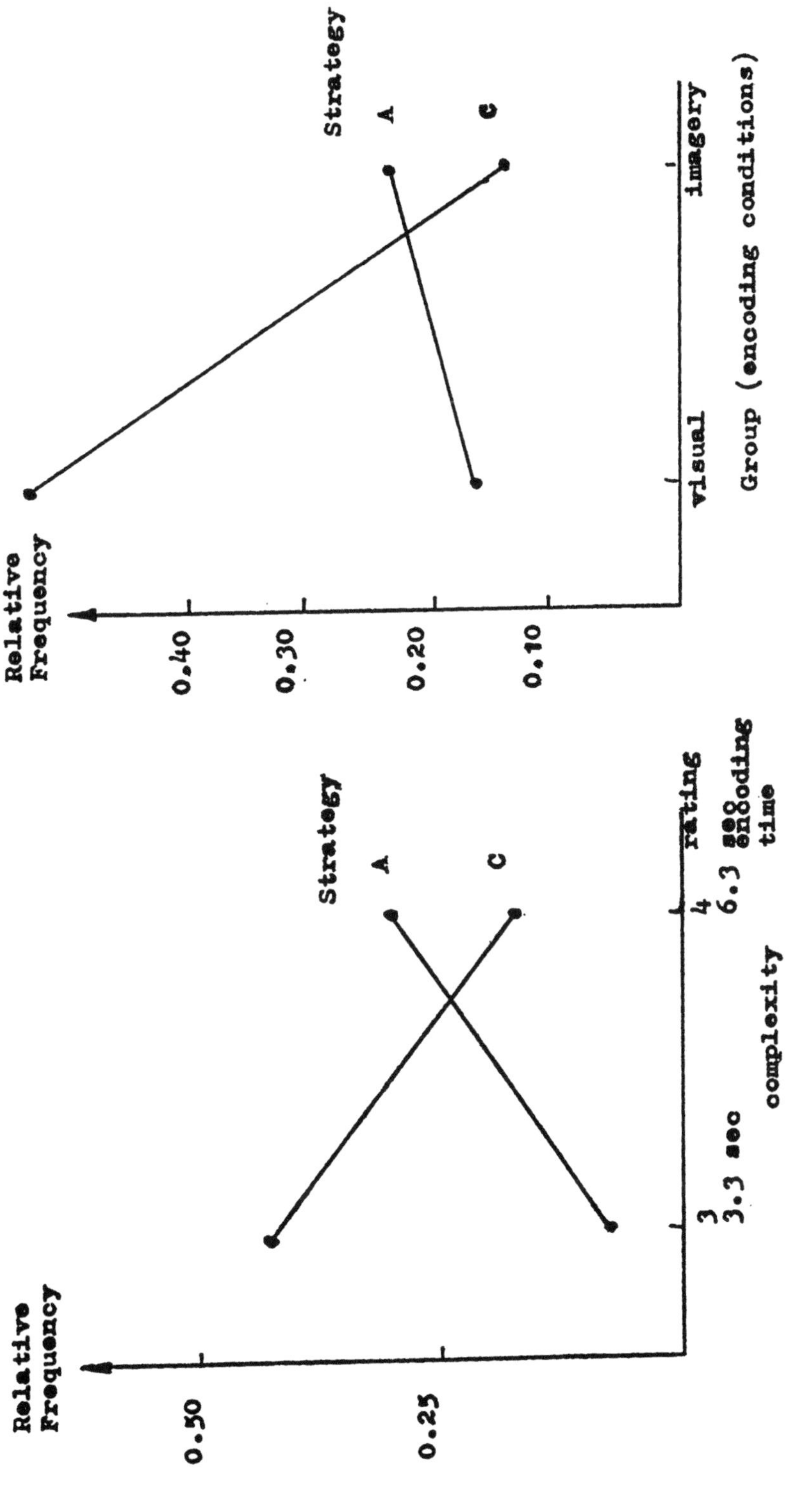

Fig. 6. Relative frequency of strategy use in dependence on (a) complexity of figures and (b) encoding conditions

Our expectation is that subjects tend to use strategy A to a greater extent in those cases where we impose more memory load (higher complex figures, drawing on the basis of information in the visual buffer).

Here are some results:

1. All the figures can be handsketched on the basis of information in the visual buffer. Less than 30 % can be programmed. This is only a hint on the reality of the mapping problem between solution plan and command sequence. A significant amount of problem solving may be required to specify the command sequence.
2. In this experiment we have to take into consideration autonomous processes of perception which result in decomposing the line drawing into part. We assume that the resulting structure is a kind of goal structure for solving the problem. We analysed the realized command sequences and compared substructures with the verbalized decompositions of the drawings. To a great extent (88,9 %) verbalized decompositions were in accordance with the internal structure of the sequence. From this data we conclude that the process of specifying the command sequence is guided by the decomposition of the drawings.
3. On figure 6 the frequency of strategy use is represented in dependence on complexity of figures and the encoding conditions. As we expected there is a interaction between these two variables and frequency of strategy use: Strategy C is used less frequently when complexity of drawings is high and when the drawings are not available during programming.

In general, the results are in accordance with our expectations. Further experiments are directed in explanning strategy use by the interaction of task variables, ability parameters and language parameters. We hope to develop a theoretical tool for understanding what the user is doing in working with graphical interfaces.

Summary

We started our investigations with the assumption, that computer-assisted problem solving process are decisive dependend on the relationship between task dependend memory structures of the problem solver and the implemented knowledge in the computer as well as the possibilities for interaction. Summarizing our first results we come to the conclusion that the problem solving process is determined by the knowledge base of the problem solver as well as the procedures and algorithms operating on this knowledge. Therefore results of memory research (Klix, 1986) are of importance for further research. As we have learned from these investigations the only possible approach for analysing complex processes such as design processes has to based on interdisciplinary research. General and differential psychology as well as engineering psychology are of relevance for this type of research. The results presented are starting points for further research which is directed on developing theoretical tools for specifying knowledge and designing man-computer interaction. Our long term goal is to contribute to the development of software tools available for the user of computers in solving problems.

References

Arndt, M.: Psychologische Untersuchungen zur Konstruktionstätigkeit. Diploma Thesis. Berlin Humboldt University 1985.

Ehrlich, K.: Soloway, E.: An empirical investigation of tacit plan knowledge in programming. In: Human Factors in Computer Systems. Eds.: Thomas J. C.; Schneider, M. L. Norwood: Ablex Publ. Comp. 1984.

Gumm, U.: Wissensabhängige Strategiebildung im interaktiven Problemlösen. Diploma Thesis. Berlin Humboldt University 1986.

Jansen, H.; Nullmeier, E.; Roediger, K. H.: Handsketching as a human factor aspect in graphical interaction. Comput. Graph. 9 (1985) 195–210.

Klix, F.: Memory research and knowledge engineering. In: Man-Machine Interaction Research. Eds.: Klix, F.; Wandke, H. Amsterdam: North-Holland 1986.

Krause, W.; Sommerfeld, E.: Neuere Ergebnisse denkpsychologischer Grundlagenforschung unter besonderer Berücksichtigung von Methodologie und Methodik in den Ingenieurwissenschaften. In: Probleme schöpferischer Ingenieurarbeit. Manuskriptdruck TH Karl-Marx-Stadt 1985.

Kyllonen, P. C.; Lohmann, D. F.; Woltz, D. J.: Componential modelling of alternative strategies for performing spatial tasks. J. Educ. Psychol. 76 (1984) 1325–1345.

Litke, P.; Lässig, K.: Zum Einfluß von Wissensstrukturen auf Programmstrukturen. Research paper. Berlin Humboldt-University 1985.

Müller, J.: Methodisch-psychologische Probleme kreativer Tätigkeit an rechnergestützten Arbeitsplätzen im modernen Konstruktionsbüro. Maschinenbautechnik 35 (1985) 224–227.

Norman, D. A.: Cognitive engineering. In: User-Centered System Design. Eds.: Norman, D. A.; Draper, S. W. Hillsdale N. J.: Erlbaum 1986.

Rich, R.: Influences of language on it's user. In: The Role of Language in Problem Solving. Eds.: Jernigon, R.; Hamill, B. W. Amsterdam: North-Holland 1985.

Seidel, E.; Kamusella, A.; Beyer, O.; Buhrand, U.: USAN, ein ESER-CAD-System zur rechnergestützten Projektierung dynamischer Antriebssysteme. Rechentechnik/Datenverarbeitung 9 (1985).

Simon, H. A.: The parameters of human memory. In: Memory and Cognitive Capabilities. Eds.: Klix F.; Hagendorf, H. Amsterdam: North-Holland 1986.

Streitz, N. A.: Cognitive ergonomics: an approach for the design of user-centered systems. In: Man-Machine-Interaction Research. Eds.: Klix, F.; Wandke, H. Amsterdam: North-Holland 1986.

Vorwerg, R.: Zum Einfluß von Wissensstrukturen auf Programmstrukturen. Research paper. Berlin Humboldt-University 1985.

Waern, Y.: Understanding learning problems in computer-aided tasks. In: Man-Machine-Interaction Research. Eds.: Klix, F.; Wandke, H. Amsterdam: North-Holland 1986.

Author's address: Dr. Elke Wetzenstein-Ollenschläger
Sektion Psychologie der Humboldt-Universität
Oranienburger Str. 18, Berlin, DDR – 1020

Bei Fragen zur Produktsicherheit wenden Sie sich bitte an:
If you have any questions regarding product safety,
please contact:

Walter de Gruyter GmbH
Genthiner Straße 13
10785 Berlin
productsafety@degruyterbrill.com